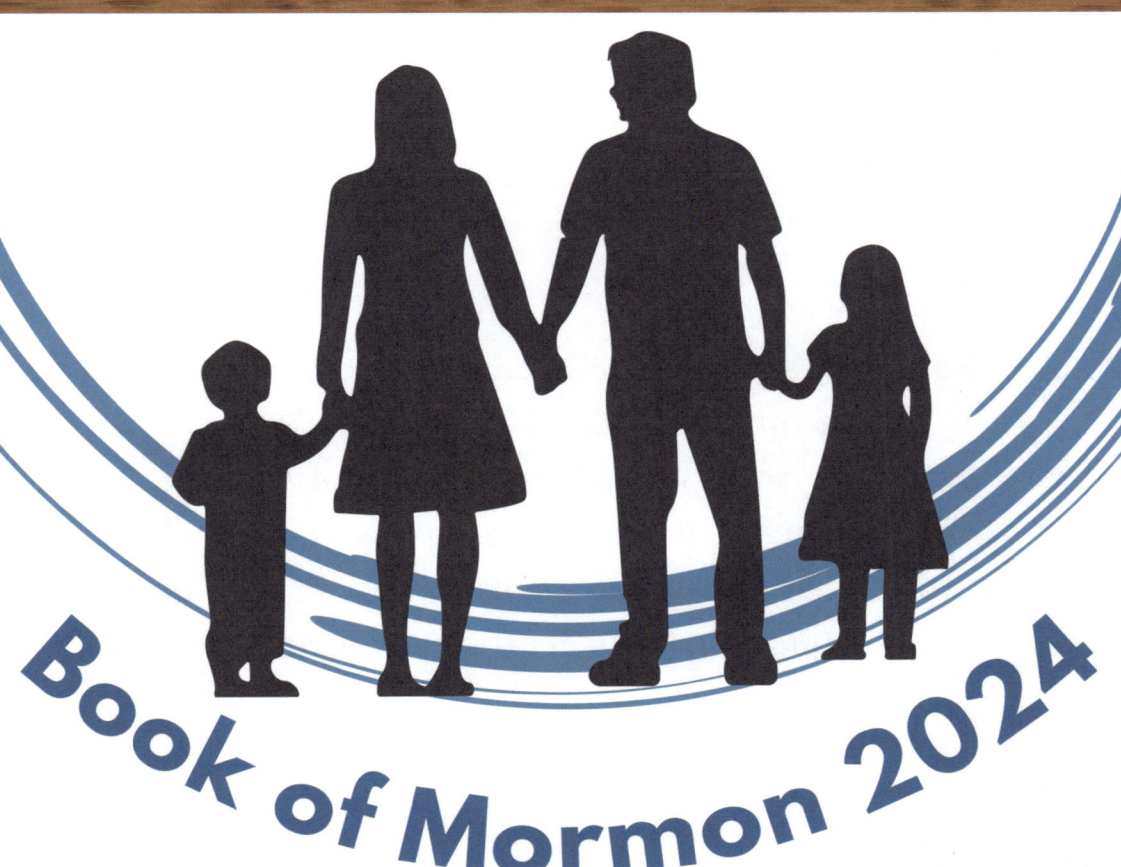

# Come Follow Me

## FAMILY HOME EVENING LESSONS

### Book of Mormon 2024

Come Follow Me Family Home Evening Lessons: Book of Mormon
2024 Copyright © 2023 by Madison Resare
All rights reserved. Printed in the United States of America. No part of this book may be used or reproduced in any manner whatsoever without written permission except in the case of brief quotations embodied in critical articles or reviews.
Book and Cover design by: Madison Resare

# Come Follow Me

**FAMILY HOME EVENING LESSONS**

## Book of Mormon 2024

CREATED BY

# Welcome!

Welcome to The Come Follow Me Family Home Evening Lessons for 2024!
This year is all about the Book of Mormon, and we can't wait to go through it with you and your family.

Each Come Follow Me lesson is broken down into an easy-to-follow Family Home Evening Lesson in this book, including spots to fill out names for scripture, prayer, songs, treats, etc., and ideas for activities, discussion questions, treats, and more.

# The Book of Mormon
## January 1-7

- Song Conductor_____
- Scripture Readers_____
- Opening Prayer_____
- Lesson_____
- Treat_____
- Closing Prayer_____

## Scriptures
Intro pages of the Book of Mormon
See also: 2 Nephi 25:26; Mosiah 3:5–8; Alma 5:48; 7:10–13; Helaman 5:12; 3 Nephi 9:13–18; 11:6–14; Moroni 10:32–33.

## Songs
"Book of Mormon Stories," Children's Songbook 118-19

## Activities
"The Book of Mormon [is] the keystone of our religion."

- Draw an Arch with a Keystone
- Use stones or blocks to create an archway. Discuss the importance of the keystone/Book of Mormon.
- What might happen if the keystone is removed? What would happen if we did not have the Book of Mormon?
- Use the Book of Mormon Reading Chart throughout 2024. (Next Page)

## Discussion Q's
If someone asked you where the Book of Mormon came from, what would you say? How would you describe God's involvement in giving us the Book of Mormon?

## Treat Suggestions
Make rice krispy treats and cut them out in rectangles to look like mini Book of Mormon books.

## Quote for the Week
The Book of Mormon is a keystone because it establishes and ties together eternal principles and precepts, rounding out basic doctrines of salvation. It is the crowning gem in the diadem of our holy scriptures.
James E. Faust

## Videos

What is the Book of Mormon

Where did the Book Come From

# Book of Mormon Reading Chart

| | | | |
|---|---|---|---|
| 1 Nephi | 2 Nephi | Jacob | Enos |
| Jarom | Omni | Words of Mormon | Moroni |
| Alma | Helaman | 3 Nephi | 4 Nephi |
| Mormon | Ether | Moroni | |

# I Will Go and Do
## January 8-14

- Song Conductor_____
- Scripture Readers_____
- Opening Prayer_____
- Lesson_____
- Treat_____
- Closing Prayer_____

## Scriptures
1 Nephi 1–5
Scriptures for little ones
(1 Nephi 3:7, 15–16)

## Songs
"As I Search the Holy Scriptures," Hymns, no. 277.

**I Will Go and Do - Song**

## Activities
- Brass Plates Scavenger Hunt - Make your own Brass plates out of spray painted cardboard or a printed picture (See picture on next page) and take turns hiding and finding the plates.
- Build a tower with some kind of blocks/legos/etc. and discuss how we build our testimonies in the same way we build towers.
- Buy a treasure chest or make one out of a cardboard box and let everyone in the family help decorate it. You can treat the scriptures like treasure by keeping them in your family treasure chest.

## Discussion Q's
- How has Jesus Christ prepared a way for each of us?
- What do you feel impressed to "go and do"?
- What are some things God has commanded us to do?
- How can we be like Nephi?

## Treat Suggestions
- Purchase some chocolate coins and eat them as you discuss how the scriptures are a treasure.
- Buy 100 Grand Bars and discuss the way Nephi put 100% into all his efforts to obtain the brass plates.
- Your family can work together to make a treat that is sort of difficult to make and have an 'I will go and do' attitude about it. (Ex: Ice Cream)

## Videos

Lehi Leaves Jerusalem

Nephi Retrieves the Plates

# Lehi's Dream
## January 15-21

- Song Conductor_____
- Scripture Readers_____
- Opening Prayer_____
- Lesson_____
- Treat_____
- Closing Prayer_____

## Scriptures

1 Nephi 6–10
For little kids: 1 Nephi 8

## Songs

"Search, Ponder, and Pray," Children's Songbook, 109;
"The Iron Rod" Hymn Book, 274

## Activities

- Tie a rope between two chairs or trees or between a couple different things in the house (make sure there is some distance and the rope is tight) Now blindfold everyone and have them hold to the rod (rope) and try to reach the end as you try to tempt them away. You can have a basket of apples to represent the fruit.
- Have each family member draw a different part of Lehi's vision then tell the story together using the pictures.
- Discuss the symbolism of items below and on the next page.

## Discussion Q's

- How do you respond when you are asked to live a gospel principle you don't understand?
- What do we learn from Lehi's vision?

## Treat Suggestions

You can try different fruits and discuss which one looks/tastes most like what you think the fruit of the tree in Lehi's vision tasted like.

## Symbolism

- Iron Rod = Word of God
- Mists of Darkness = Temptation
- Field = World
- River = Hell
- Spacious Building = Pride
- Tree = Love of God

## Videos

Lord Delivers Nephi from Brothers

Lehi Sees a Vision of the Tree

Iron Rod = Word of God

Mists of Darkness = Temptation

Field = World

River = Hell

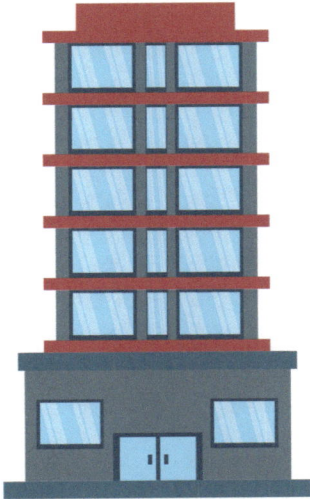
Spacious Building = Pride

Tree = Love of God

# Nephi's Vision
## January 22-28

- Song Conductor_____
- Scripture Readers_____
- Opening Prayer_____
- Lesson_____
- Treat_____
- Closing Prayer_____

## Scriptures
1 Nephi 11–15
Little Kids: 1 Nephi 11:16–33

## Songs
"He Sent His Son" (Children's Songbook, 34–35)
"The Iron Rod" Hymn Book, 274

## Activities
- Cut out the Symbols from the previous lesson and hid them around the house for a Tree of Life Scavenger hunt. Once all the symbols are found discuss them and see who can remember what they represent.
- As a family, paint/color/decorate the cover of a Book of Mormon for your family to use throughout the year.

(The Book of Mormon restores gospel truths lost during the Apostasy.)

## Discussion Q's
- What are some of the great and marvelous things God has done for you?
- How does the Savior help you avoid—and escape from—the captivity of false ideas?
- What do you think it means to "hold fast" to the scriptures and words of living prophets?
- What might it mean to "hold fast" to Jesus Christ?
- What "plain and precious" truths have you learned from the Book of Mormon?

## Treat Suggestions
As a family dip pretzel rods in chocolate, then decorate with sprinkles, chocolate drizzles, etc. These can represent the rod of iron and will be a tasty treat!

## Videos

Nephi sees a Vision

A Book From God

# I Will Prepare the Way
## January 29–February 4

- Song Conductor_____
- Scripture Readers_____
- Opening Prayer_____
- Lesson_____
- Treat_____
- Closing Prayer_____

## Scriptures

1 Nephi 16–22
Little Kids: 1 Nephi 17:3

## Songs

"Where Can I Turn for Peace?" (Hymns, no. 129)
"Nephi's Courage" (Children's Songbook, 120–21).

## Activities

- Create a Map/Hunt your children can accomplish using a compass. Discuss the similarities between the compass and the Liahona.
- Use blankets, cardboard, chairs, beds, couches and have your kids build their own boat.
- Draw pictures of what you think the boat looked like when it was finished.

## Discussion Q's

- What can you learn from Nephi about facing adversity with faith in Jesus Christ?
- What similarities do you see between the Liahona and the Holy Ghost?

## Treat Suggestions

Boat Snack
Get clear plastic cups and make a batch of blue Jello. Pour the Jello into the cups and allow them to set. The blue Jello will be the ocean. Use small orange sections as the boat and use toothpicks and fruit roll-up/leather as the sails.

## Videos

The Lord Guides Lehi's Journey

The Lord Tells Nephi to Build a Boat

Lehi's Family Sails to the Promised Land

He Will Give You Help (Extra Video)

# Free to Choose
## February 5 - 11

- Song Conductor_____
- Scripture Readers_____
- Opening Prayer_____
- Lesson_____
- Treat_____
- Closing Prayer_____

## Scriptures
2 Nephi 1–2
Little Kids: 2 Nephi 2:27 (Choices)

## Songs
"Know This, That Every Soul Is Free," Hymns, no. 240.
"Choose the Right" (Hymns, no. 239).

## Activities
- Print the two faces on the next page and cut them out. Then write on a board, piece of paper different choices we make in this life and let your children decide whether those choices would make God happy or sad.
- Give your child one pencil and tell them to break it. It should break easily. Then give them more pencils as you list out-loud different choices that could be hard to make better. Once they have a stack of pencils ask if they can break them all at once. It is harder to break once we have a whole stack of bad choices.

## Discussion Q's
- Why is agency so important?
- How does correctly understanding the Fall help us better understand our need for Jesus Christ?
- What choices help us stay connected to God?
- How is sin like a chain?

## Treat Suggestions
Buy a box of assorted chocolates. Let everyone pick one (with no indication of what is inside.) Making choices without the help of God is a lot like guessing which chocolates might taste good. Then give them the list or map of what is inside each chocolate and explain that God gives us a road map to making good choices.

## Quote for the Week
Know this, that ev'ry soul is free
To choose his life and what he'll be…"
Hymn no. 240.

# The Manner of Happiness
## February 12-18

- Song Conductor_____
- Scripture Readers_____
- Opening Prayer_____
- Lesson_____
- Treat_____
- Closing Prayer_____

## Scriptures

2 Nephi 3–5
Little Kids: 2 Nephi 4:35

## Songs

"I Love to See the Temple," Children's Songbook, 95).

## Activities

- Read 2 Nephi 5:27 and discuss the different ways we can live after the manner of happiness.
- Read 2 Nephi 5:15–16 then work together or split into teams and build your own Temples using blocks, legos, or sugar cubes.
- Take a piece of paper and a pen and take turns adding to one drawing of a Temple. See how it looks at the end.

## Discussion Q's

- Why was Joseph Smith Important?
- Why is the Book of Mormon Important?
- What do you think it means to live after the manner of happiness?

## Treat Suggestions

Make a temple out of mini, and or large marshmallows. Then eat your creation!

## Quote for the Week

I testify to you that the temples are sacred, holy places. They are a source of spiritual power and strength. They are a place of revelation. They are the house of the Lord." Silvia H. Allred

## Holiday

Celebrate Valentine's by cutting out the hearts provided (next page) and writing acts of service on them, draw one heart a day and perform the service.

## Videos

Till We All Come in the Unity of Faith

# The Plan of God
## February 19 - 25

- Song Conductor _____
- Scripture Readers _____
- Opening Prayer _____
- Lesson _____
- Treat _____
- Closing Prayer _____

## Scriptures
2 Nephi 6–10
Little Kids: 2 Nephi 9:21–22

## Songs
"How Great Thou Art" (Hymns, no. 86).
"I Feel My Savior's Love" (Children's Songbook, 74–75)

## Activities
- Discuss why you are grateful for Jesus Christ.
- Have everyone in the family draw a picture of a pit and a ladder. The pit represents sin and Jesus not only gave us a ladder (resurrection) but he went down into the pit (suffered for our sins) and shows us how to climb out. All we have to do is follow His example.

## Discussion Q's
- What do we receive from Christ's atonement?
- What do we know about God's plan?
- How do we know God loves us?
- Why is it important to trust God's counsel even if we do not completely understand it
- How do we rely on God instead of on our own understanding?

## Treat Suggestion
Provide each family member with nine pennies and then lay out an assortment of candies/snacks that are all listed for 10 cents. Explain that the treats represent eternal life, and on our own we can't reach it/pay for it. But God makes up the difference. Give everyone an extra penny so they can purchase their treat.

## Videos

Where Justice and Mercy Meet

Jacob Teaches

Jacob Encourages the Nephites

# Prince of Peace
## February 26 - March 3

- Song Conductor_____
- Scripture Readers_____
- Opening Prayer_____
- Lesson_____
- Treat_____
- Closing Prayer_____

## Scriptures
2 Nephi 11–19
Little Kids 2 Nephi 19:2

## Songs
"High on the Mountain Top," Hymns, no 5.
"I Love to See the Temple" (Children's Songbook, 95).

## Activities
- Find a flashlight/lantern/candle and let everyone take a turn trying to walk in the dark vs. walking with a light then read 2 Nephi 19:2 and discuss how the light is a symbol for Jesus Christ.
- Read 2 Nephi 19:6 together and list all the things Jesus has been called/is known for. Discuss which ones are your favorites.
- Have your kids draw pictures of your family going to the temple.

## Discussion Q's
Read 2 Nephi 12:2 Why is a mountain a good symbol for the temple?

## Treat Suggestions
Try making rice Krispy treats in the shapes of lightbulbs and discuss how Christ is a light for us as you eat them.

## Videos
The video to the right that shows different people seeing Jesus for the first time. Discuss what these people might have felt. What would we feel? How will we feel when we see Him again?

The Christ Child

# We Rejoice in Christ
## March 4 - 10

- Song Conductor _____
- Scripture Readers _____
- Opening Prayer _____
- Lesson _____
- Treat _____
- Closing Prayer _____

## Scriptures
2 Nephi 20–25
For Little Kids: 2 Nephi 25:26

## Songs
"I Believe in Christ" (Hymns, no. 134)

## Activities
- Read 2 Nephi 21:6-7 and have your kids draw pictures of the animals getting along together.
- Or color and cut the animal pictures on the next two pages, then on a new piece of paper draw a happy peaceful scene and glue the animals to the scene.
- Read 2 Nephi 21:11–12) and talk about how Ensigns are like flags. Have everyone in the family draw their own flag that represents the things they love and believe in.

## Discussion Q's
- What does it mean to be a peacemaker?
- How can you help keep peace in your home?
- How does the Savior bring you joy?
- What can you share about Jesus with others?
- How can you share that joy with others?

## Treat Suggestions
Make sugar cookies and cut them into the shapes of different animals that normally don't get along.

## Quote for the Week
"Peacemakers are not passive; they are persuasive in the Savior's way. What gives us the inner strength to cool, calm, and quench the fiery darts aimed toward the truths we love? The strength comes from our faith in Jesus Christ and our faith in His words."
— Neil L. Andersen

## Videos

**Jesus Heals Man Born Blind**

**Suffer the little children to come unto me.**

# Work and a Wonder
## March 11 - 17

- Song Conductor_____
- Scripture Readers_____
- Opening Prayer_____
- Lesson_____
- Treat_____
- Closing Prayer_____

## Scriptures

2 Nephi 26–30
For little kids: 2 Nephi 28:2

## Songs

"Come unto Jesus" (Hymns, no. 117)
"I'll Walk with You" (Children's Songbook, 140–41),

## Activities

- Read 2 Nephi 28 verses verses 5, 6, 8, 21–23, 29 and look for the different ways Satan will lead people astray.
- Discuss as a family what you can do when Satan is trying to deceive you.
- What would you say to someone who said, "we already have the Bible, we don't need anything else."?
- Read 2 Nephi 28:30 then build a puzzle together and talk about how God gives his children truth little by little.

## Discussion Q's

- Why is the Book of Mormon so Important?
- How do receive more 'Word' from God?
- Are we ready to receive revelation?

## Treat Suggestions

Bake something together as a family and read the instructions line by line, like God gives instruction.

## Quote for the Week

"What has Jesus Christ done for each of us? He has done everything that is essential for our journey through mortality toward the destiny outlined in the plan of our Heavenly Father."

Dallin H. Oaks

# This is the Way
## March 18 - 24

- Song Conductor _____
- Scripture Readers _____
- Opening Prayer _____
- Lesson _____
- Treat _____
- Closing Prayer _____

## Scriptures

2 Nephi 31–33
Little Kids: Matthew 3:13–17).

## Songs

"Did You Think to Pray?" (Hymns, no. 140).

## Activities

- Talk about what it means to feast on the word of Christ. You can offer some of your kids' favorite foods or treats and a few of their least favorite ones to showcase the difference.
- Read 2 Nephi 32:8–9 and talk about why we should pray always. Draw pictures of different situations that would be especially good to pray through..

## Discussion Q's

- Why was Christ baptized?
- Why are we baptized?
- What promises are made at baptism?
- How can you make sure the Holy Ghost is always with you?

## Treat Suggestions

Some favorite foods and treats.

## Quote for the Week

"To feast means to savor. We savor the scriptures by studying them in a spirit of delightful discovery and faithful obedience."
President Russell M. Nelson,

## Videos

Daily Bread Pattern

Nephi Records Final Testimony

# He is Not Here, For He is Risen

## March 25 - 31

- Song Conductor _____
- Scripture Readers _____
- Opening Prayer _____
- Lesson _____
- Treat _____
- Closing Prayer _____

## Scriptures
Jacob 4:3–4).
Luke 24:36–43

## Songs
"I Know That My Redeemer Lives" (Hymns, no. 136)

---

### See Following Easter Activity Pages for FHE/Home Decor/Activity/Treat Ideas

### Contents:
- **He is Risen - Home Decor**
- **Easter Coloring Book**
- **Easter Family Home Evening**
- **Easter Treat**

# HE IS NOT HERE
## For He is
# RISEN

Matthew 28:6

# Easter Story

**JOHN 13:3-17**

PAGE 2

**MARK 14:22-26**

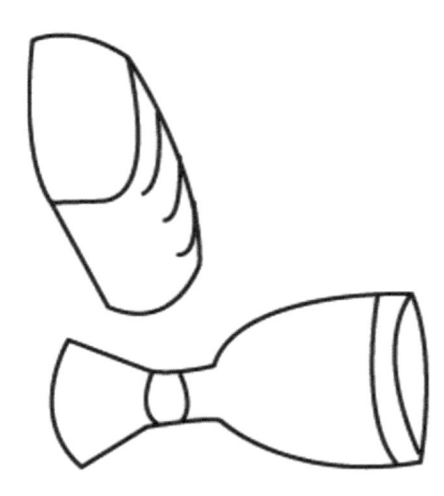

PAGE 3

**MATTHEW 21:1-9**

PAGE 1

MATTHEW 26:14-16

PAGE 4

MATTHEW 27:35

PAGE 6

MATTHEW 27:29-31

PAGE 5

JOHN 19:16-17

PAGE 7

# Easter Family Home Evening

**Hold This Family Home Evening on Easter Eve or some time on Easter Sunday to center your celebrations on Christ.**

## Song: Easter Hosanna

## Scripture: Matthew 26-28

"He is not here: for he is risen, as he said. Come, see the place where the Lord lay."

- Matthew 28:6

## Lesson/Activity:

### Activities:
1. Color, cut out and staple the Easter story printable (included in this packet) as a family. Then, use the scriptures/pictures included in the story to talk about the Resurrection.
2. Take turns opening the Resurrection Easter Eggs (printable included in this packet) and discuss the symbolism behind each object.
3. Read the scriptures about the Resurrection and act it out as a family.

### Questions to Ask:
- How has Christ made a difference in your life?
- Why is He important to you?
- Why is it significant that the Savior's sacrifice occurred simultaneously as Passover?

## Treat:

Make Resurrection Easter Cookies the night before Easter. Instructions on next page.

# Resurrection Easter Cookies

## Ingredients:

- 1 cup pecan halves
- 1 teaspoon distilled white vinegar
- 3 egg whites
- 1 pinch salt
- 1 cup white sugar

## Directions:

1. Preheat oven to 300 degrees F (150 degrees C).
2. Place pecans in a resealable plastic baggie. Crush the pecans into small bits. (Read John 19:1-3)
3. Put 1 teaspoon vinegar into a medium bowl. (Read John 19:28-30)
4. Add egg whites to the vinegar. (Read John 10:10-11)
5. Sprinkle salt into the egg whites. (Read Luke 23:27)
6. Add 1 cup sugar. (Read Psalm 34:8 and John 3:16.) Beat with mixer on high speed for 12 to 15 minutes until stiff peaks are formed. (Read Isaiah 1:18 and John 3:1-3.)
7. Fold in broken nuts. Drop by teaspoons onto a parchment paper-lined baking sheet. (Read Matthew 27:57-60.)
8. Place cookies in the oven, close the door, and turn the oven off. (Read Matthew 27:65-66.)
9. Go to bed. (Read John 16:20 and 22.)
10. In the morning, open the oven and take out the cookies. (Read Matthew 28:1-9.)

The cookies should be hollow inside to represent the tomb being empty.

# Sharing with Others
## April 1-7

- Song Conductor_____
- Scripture Readers_____
- Opening Prayer_____
- Lesson_____
- Treat_____
- Closing Prayer_____

## Scriptures
Jacob 1–4,
Little Kids: Jacob 2:13 and 2 Nephi 10:24.

## Songs
"Because I Have Been Given Much"
(Hymns, no. 219)

## Activities
- God helps heal our wounds. Discuss what this means with your children using medicine and bandaids, as props.
- Read Jacob 2:17 and discuss the importance of sharing what we have with others. What would happen if everyone shared their skills, and wealth?
- Share a treat! Suggestions below.

## Discussion Q's
- How should we view material wealth?
- What should we do or how should we behave when we are blessed with much?
- What are the blessings of living a chaste life?

## Story for the Week
Matthew 7:24-27 (Wise man and the Foolish man)

## Treat Suggestions
Make a treat like cupcakes, bread, cookies, cake, etc. and have your kids split up the treats to share with everyone. Maybe you could make enough of your treat to share with a neighbor or friend as well.

## Videos

Spiritual Whirlwinds

I Choose to be Pure

# The Lord Labors with Us

## April 8-14

- Song Conductor _____
- Scripture Readers _____
- Opening Prayer _____
- Lesson _____
- Treat _____
- Closing Prayer _____

## Scriptures

Jacob 5–7
For kids: Jacob 5:70–75

## Songs

"Israel, Israel, God Is Calling," Hymns, no. 7;
"Stand for the Right," Children's Songbook, 159.

## Activities

- As a family, make a list of things you can all do to help gather Israel.

- Explain the story of the olive tree or watch the allegory of the Olive Tree for Kids video (QR code below) and have everyone draw a picture of what they have learned.

## Discussion Q's

- How can we help others' feel the Savior's love?
- What does Jesus do to show that He cares for us?

## Treat Suggestions

Because you are discussing olive trees, your family could try out different kinds of olives, maybe have some other fruits from trees as well, in case the olives are not a favorite.

## Quote for the Week

Repentance is real and it works. It is not a fictional experience or the product "of a frenzied mind." It has the power to lift burdens and replace them with hope. It can lead to a mighty change of heart that results in our having "no more disposition to do evil, but to do good continually."
- Elder Allen D. Haynie

## Videos

Jacob Teaches Olive Tree Allegory

Allegory of the Olive Tree for Kids

# According to His Will
## April 15-21

- Song Conductor _____
- Scripture Readers _____
- Opening Prayer _____
- Lesson _____
- Treat _____
- Closing Prayer _____

## Scriptures
Enos - Words of Mormon
Kids: Enos 1:1–17

## Songs
"Sweet Hour of Prayer," Hymns, no. 142.
"A Child's Prayer" (Children's Songbook, 12–13).

## Quote for the Week

"Whatever problems your family is facing, whatever you must do to solve them, the beginning and the end of the solution is charity, the pure love of Christ. Without this love, even seemingly perfect families struggle. With it, even families with great challenges succeed.

'Charity never faileth.'

It is true for saving marriages! It is true for saving families!"
"In Praise of Those Who Save" (Ensign or Liahona, May 2016, 77–80).

## Discussion Q's

- What example does Enos show us?
- How can we learn to pray from Enos?
- How can our family come unto Christ?
- How can we make our prayers more meaningful?
- Imagine you are talking to God face to face - what would you want to talk about?
- Discuss the different ways the Lord answers prayers.
- Have you ever been inspired to do something kind for someone else?

## Videos

Enos Prays Mightily

Home and Family

# Filled with Love
## April 22-28

- Song Conductor _____
- Scripture Readers _____
- Opening Prayer _____
- Lesson _____
- Treat _____
- Closing Prayer _____

## Scriptures

Mosiah 1-3
Kids: Mosiah 2:17, Matthew 25:40

## Songs

"A Poor Wayfaring Man of Grief" (Hymns, no. 29)

## Activities

King Benjamin is an excellent example of how a King should be. Use the crown template on the next page to make your own crowns. Then think of ways your family can serve each other.

## Treat Ideas

Use sugar cookie dough and cut/shape it into crowns - use an upside down cupcake tin to mold them and keep their upright crown shape.

## Discussion Q's

- How is your life better because of the scriptures?
- Read Mosiah 2:10-26 and discuss how King Benjamin served his people and how we can follow his example.
- Why do we keep the commandments?
- How does Jesus Christ help us overcome sin?

## Videos

Overcoming Adversity

The Old Shoemaker

King Benjamin Teaches

# A Mighty Change
## April 29 - May 5

- **Song Conductor** _____
- **Scripture Readers** _____
- **Opening Prayer** _____
- **Lesson** _____
- **Treat** _____
- **Closing Prayer** _____

## Scriptures
Mosiah 4–6
For kids: Mosiah 4:1-3, Mosiah 5: 7-9

## Songs
"I Know My Father Lives," Hymns, no. 302.
"I'll Walk with You," Children's Songbook, 140–41)

## Activities
- Compare and discuss how it feels when your hands are dirty vs clean. for young children you can have them get their hands dirty with dirt and sticky things then wash them off as you discuss.
- Read Mosiah 4:26 and discuss the different ways your family could serve the poor and the needy.

## Discussion Q's
- What does it mean to take upon yourself the name of Christ?

## Treat Suggestions
Read Mosiah 5:12 and discuss how you can put Christ's name on your hearts. As you make heart-shaped cookies, write the name 'Christ' on top in edible frosting/sprinkles/etc.

## Videos

Christlike Attributes

A Change of Heart

The people of King Benjamin Make a Covenant

# Prophets, Seers, and Revelators
## May 6-12

- Song Conductor_____
- Scripture Readers_____
- Opening Prayer_____
- Lesson_____
- Treat_____
- Closing Prayer_____

## Scriptures

Mosiah 7-10
For kids: Mosiah 7:1, 7:33

## Songs

"Book of Mormon Stories" or "Nephi's Courage"
(Children's Songbook, 118–19, 120–21)

## Activities

- Discuss how our choices can affect others for good or bad - especially those close to us. Set up a line of dominoes and watch how knocking down one can affect the rest.
- Read Moses 6:35–36 and discuss the importance of Seers. You can use things like binoculars/glasses/telescopes/microscopes as examples of things that help us 'see' things other people cannot.

## Discussion Q's

- Read Mosiah 8:18 and discuss how the apostles and prophets have blessed and guided us today.
- We heard from the Prophets and apostle last month, what stood out to you? What inspired you?

## Treat Suggestions

"Book of Mormon Stories," Children's Songbook 118-19

## Fun

Cut out the footprints on the following pages, have your children write or draw pictures of some things the Prophets have counseled us to do. Lay the footprints in a line or circle and have the whole family step on/follow the footprints as you all sing 'Follow the Prophet' (Children's Songbook 110)

# Keep the Commandments
## May 13-19

- Song Conductor_____
- Scripture Readers_____
- Opening Prayer_____
- Lesson_____
- Treat_____
- Closing Prayer_____

## Scriptures
Mosiah 11-17
For Kids: Mosiah 16:9

## Songs
"Do What Is Right" or "Let Us All Press On" (Hymns, nos. 237, 243). "Keep the Commandments" (Children's Songbook, 146–47).

## Activities
- Read Mosiah 13:11-26 And discuss as a family how you can engrave the commandments of God into your hearts. Use the heart-shaped cutouts in the following pages to write the commandments, cut them out, and display them in your home.
- What blessings can come from obeying the commandments?

## Discussion Q's
Watch the video 'Abinidi Testifies' by using the QR code below then discuss how we can try to be brave like Abinidi.

## Treat Suggestions
Buy a favorite candy/treat and have everyone in the family take turns listing the different commandments - each right answer gets a treat.

## Quote for the Week
Courage is required to make an initial thrust toward one's coveted goal, but even greater courage is called for when one stumbles and must make a second effort to achieve.

("Chapter 8: The Call for Courage," Teachings of Presidents of the Church: Thomas S. Monson (2022), 135–47)

## Videos

Abinidi Testifies

Dare to Stand Alone

# Commandments/Covenants
## May 20-26

- Song Conductor_____
- Scripture Readers_____
- Opening Prayer_____
- Lesson_____
- Treat_____
- Closing Prayer_____

## Scriptures

Mosiah 18-24
For Kids: Mosiah 18:19, 18:14,

## Songs

"Keep the Commandments," Children's Songbook, 146–47.
"Love One Another," Hymns, no. 308.

## Activities/Questions

- Read Mosiah 18:8-10 together and talk about the things we promise to do when we are baptized - keep the commandments, serve others, etc.
- What does God promise you at baptism?
- Read Mosiah 18:19 and discuss what it means to stand as a witness for God.
- For those who have been baptized talk about your experiences. Prepare those who are not yet old enough.

## Treat Suggestions

**Nutter Butter 10 Commandments**

Ingredients:
- Nutter Butter Cookies
- White Melting Chocolate
- Black Melting Chocolate
- Toothpicks

Instructions:
1. Melt the white chocolate with one or two black chocolates to make a grey color and dip the nutter butters to coat.
2. Use toothpicks to connect two nutter butters together side by side to look like stone tablets.
3. Set aside to dry.
4. Melt the black chocolate.
5. Use a toothpick to add the 10 commandments - use roman numerals and squigly lines to look more authentic.

## Videos

Alma Teaches/Baptizes

# Born Again/Conversion
## May 27–June 2

- Song Conductor _____
- Scripture Readers _____
- Opening Prayer _____
- Lesson _____
- Treat _____
- Closing Prayer _____

## Scriptures
Mosiah 25-28
Kids: Mosiah 26:1-6, 27:14

## Songs
"I Stand All Amazed"? (*Hymns*, no. 193).
"Help Me, Dear Father," Children's Songbook, 99.)

## Questions

- Read Mosiah 27:14, and discuss. What does it mean that our prayers might be answered according to our faith?
- How does the Savior help us to change? or be born again?
- Read Mosiah 26:29-31, What do these verses teach us about forgiving others?
- Fill a bag with rocks and discuss the importance of forgiveness, each time we forgive or ask for forgiveness the Lord lightens our burdens - take a rock out of the bag as you lighten the load and take turns carrying the bag as it gets lighter - discuss.

## Activity
Pray and fast for the Lord to bless someone in your family who is struggling.

## Treat Suggestions
Make a desert like cookies, brownies, rice Krispies, or even strawberries and cut them out to look like hearts - discuss the mighty change of heart Alma the Younger went through.

## Videos

Alma the Younger Testifies

## Quote for the Week
Through faith in Christ, we can be spiritually prepared and cleansed from sin, immersed in and saturated with His gospel, and purified and sealed by the Holy Spirit of Promise. (David A. Bednar Ensign or Liahona, May 2007, 19–22).

# Kindness Begins with Me

## June 3-9

- Song Conductor_____
- Scripture Readers_____
- Opening Prayer_____
- Lesson_____
- Treat_____
- Closing Prayer_____

## Scriptures

Mosiah 29-Alma 4
Kids: Alma 1:19-30

## Songs

"Testimony," Hymns, no. 137;
"Kindness Begins with Me" (Children's Songbook, 145),

## Questions/Activities

- Read Alma 1:19-30 and discuss. Ask your family - How do true followers of Jesus Christ feel about people who have different beliefs?
- How should we think about or treat wealth/riches/prosperity?
- Read Alma 4:19 - Discuss the importance of pure testimony. Practice sharing your testimonies with your family.
- Make a list of ways your family could serve and be kind to others after singing 'Kindness begins with me..'

## Treat Suggestions

As you talk about wealth and prosperity, you can hand your children chocolate coins and have them talk about the different (good/kind/nice) things they would and can do with their own blessings/prosperity. Also, discuss the importance of accepting help when it is needed - sometimes you will be on the receiving end of service and when that happens you are allowing others to receive blessings from God by serving you. Accept service from others with gratitude and humility and know that it takes courage and a strong heart to accept help.

## Videos

Alma steps down as chief judge

## Quote for the Week

"I invite you to seek opportunities to bear your testimony in word and in deed."
Gary E. Stevenson, "Nourishing and Bearing Your Testimony," *Liahona*, Nov. 2022, 111–14;

# Mighty Change of Heart

## June 10-16

- Song Conductor_____
- Scripture Readers_____
- Opening Prayer_____
- Lesson_____
- Treat_____
- Closing Prayer_____

## Scriptures

Alma 5-7
Kids: Alma 7:15

## Songs

"I Need Thee Every Hour" or "I Know That My Redeemer Lives" (Hymns, nos. 98, 136)

## Questions/Activities

- Read Alma 5:14 together and discuss what it means to be spiritually born of God? What it means to have His image in your countenance? And If you have experienced a mighty change in your heart?
- Sing "I'm Trying to Be like Jesus" (*Children's Songbook*, 78–79) together then discuss how you are all trying to be like Jesus

## Activity

M. Russell Ballard said: "I need to regularly take time to ask myself, 'How am I doing?' Like a personal interview. Take the interview on the following page to check in with how you are doing according to Alma 5:14-33.

## Quote for the Week

"To endure to the end, we need to be eager to please God and worship Him with fervor and passion. This means that we maintain faith in Jesus Christ by praying, studying the scriptures, partaking of the sacrament each week, and having the Holy Ghost as our constant companion. We need to actively help and serve others and share the gospel with them. We need to be perfectly upright and honest in all things, never compromising our covenants with God or our commitments to men, regardless of circumstances."
- Dale G. Renlund, "Preserving the Heart's Mighty Change," Ensign or Liahona, Nov. 2009, 97–99.

# Personal Interview

Read Alma 5:14-33 journal your answers to the following questions:

- Have ye spiritually been born of God? _____

- Have ye received his image in your countenance? _____

- Have ye experienced a mighty change in your heart? _____

- Do ye exercise faith in God? _____

- Do you look forward with an eye of faith? _____

- Are you ready to be judged according to your deeds? _____

- Can you imagine the Lord saying to you, "Come unto me ye blessed, for behold, your works of righteousness upon the face of the earth? _____

- Can ye look up to God at the Last day with a pure heart and clean hands
_____

- If you were to die at this time, within yourselves could ye say that ye have been sufficiently humble? _____

- Could you say that your garments have been cleansed and made white through the blood of Christ, who will come to redeem his people from their sins?
_____

- Are ye stripped of pride? _____

- Are you ready to meet God? _____

- Have you repented of your sins? _____

# Plan of Redemption
## June 17-23

- Song Conductor_____
- Scripture Readers_____
- Opening Prayer_____
- Lesson_____
- Treat_____
- Closing Prayer_____

## Scriptures

Alma 8-12
Kids: Alma 8:18

## Songs

"Help Me Teach with Inspiration," Hymns, no. 281;
"I Want to Be a Missionary Now" (Children's Songbook, 168)

## Questions/Activities

- Look up the word 'Redemption' and discuss why the word 'redemption' is used to describe God's plan.
- What other words do you know that have been used to describe God's plan? Why do you think those words were used?
- How can we share the gospel with our friends and family?
- Can you think of a time when someone was a good friend to you?
- What about a time when you were a good friend?

## Activity

Make a friendship puzzle or friendship bracelets and give them to your friends.

## Treat Suggestions

If you do not have the time to make friendship bracelets maybe you could get some candy friendship bracelets and give those out to your friends.

## Videos

Alma Commanded to Return

Amulek Testifies of Jesus Christ

Alma Warns Zeezrom

# Change/Personal Growth

## June 24-30

- Song Conductor_____
- Scripture Readers_____
- Opening Prayer_____
- Lesson_____
- Treat_____
- Closing Prayer_____

## Scriptures

Alma 13-16
Kids: Alma 15:3-12

## Songs

"Come unto Jesus," Hymns, no. 117.
"When I Am Baptized" (Children's Songbook, 103)

## Questions/Discussion

- The Priesthood is the ability to use God's power on earth. Read Matthew 26:26–28; Mark 5:22–24, 35–43; while you look for different ways the Priesthood power is used.
- How can your family benefit from the Priesthood power?
    - What are ordinances? Read Alma 13:16 and discuss the importance of these ordinances.
    - Scan this QR code for a list of ordinances

## Activity

Read Alma 15:3-12 and talk about how Zeezrom changed and watch the video below.

## Treat Suggestions

Make cookies or a cake together as a family. Discuss how baking is an act of faith. You do everything you know how to do - follow the instructions and do your best to combine the ingredients the right way, then you put it in the oven and it changes into something edible. Just like our lives - we try to follow God's instructions, we live the best way we know how, and we exercise faith. God helps us to change into something better, something more than we can be without him.

Just like cookies going in an oven - sometimes we face hard trials that shape us/change us into something better.

## Videos

Zeezrom is Healed/Baptized

# Share the Gospel
## July 1-7

- 🔵 Song Conductor _____
- 🟠 Scripture Readers _____
- 🔵 Opening Prayer _____

- 🟠 Lesson _____
- 🔵 Treat _____
- 🟠 Closing Prayer _____

## Scriptures

Alma 17-22
Kids: Alma 22:15,18

## Songs

"Brightly Beams Our Father's Mercy," Hymns, no. 335; "Called to Serve" (Children's Songbook, 174–75).

## Activities

Watch the video here

Now discuss the importance of sharing the gospel. How can your family share the gospel?

## Discussion Q's

Read Alma 17:11 How can we be a good example to others? How can we be instruments for the Lord?

## Treat Suggestions

Make a treat to share with friends and neighbors and include a message of love/appreciation from the gospel. You can use one of the examples on the next page.

## Videos

Come and See

Come and Help

Come and Belong

# GOD IS AMONG US

DIETER F. UCHTDORF

---

# GOD IS AMONG US

DIETER F. UCHTDORF

# They Never did Fall Away

## July 8-14

- Song Conductor _____
- Scripture Readers _____
- Opening Prayer _____
- Lesson _____
- Treat _____
- Closing Prayer _____

## Scriptures
Alma 23-29
Kids: Alma 23:7

## Songs
Jesus, Lover of My Soul," Hymns, no. 102.
I Want to Live the Gospel" (Children's Songbook, 148)

## Activities/Discussion

- Read Alma 26:5-7 and ponder what the sheaves, garners, and storm might represent in your life.

- Read Alma 24:6, 18 and discuss what it means that they were willing to bury their weapons of war. How can we show that kind of example? How do we show our commitment to being Christlike and following God?

- Draw pictures of the things in the gospel that bring you joy.

- The Nephites helped the Anti-Nephi-Lehi's to keep their promise to never take up arms again by protecting them. How can we help our friends to keep their promises?

## Quote for the Week

"Sharing the gospel is not a burden but a joy. What we call "member missionary work" is not a program but an attitude of love and outreach to help those around us. It is also an opportunity to witness how we feel about the restored gospel of our Savior."

Dallin H. Oaks (*Ensign* or *Liahona*, Nov. 2016, 57–60).

## Videos

Sharing Your Beliefs

Sharing the Gospel

# The Word of God
## July 15-21

- Song Conductor_____
- Scripture Readers_____
- Opening Prayer_____
- Lesson_____
- Treat_____
- Closing Prayer_____

## Scriptures
Alma 30-31
Alma 31:9, 11

## Songs
Oh Say, What Is Truth?," Hymns, no. 272.
My Heavenly Father Loves Me" (Children's Songbook, 228–29),

## Discussions
- Read Alma 30:6-31 together and discuss the different false teachings of Korihor. How would they sound pleasing to others?
- How can you tell when something is fake vs true?
- Read all about the Word of God in these verses (Alma 31:5 Hebrews 4:12; 1 Nephi 15:23–24; 2 Nephi 31:20; Jacob 2:8; Helaman 3:29–30).

## More Discussions
Read Alma 30:6 and discuss what an Anti-Christ is and what it means.
Read Alma 30:44 and discuss what it means that 'all things denote there is a God.'

## Treat
There are a few different candies that work like bricks - candy lego bricks work especially well. You can use these to build edible rameumptoms.

## Activity
Watch the video about the Zoramites and the Rameumptom by scanning the QR code here.

As a family, build a Rameumptom tower with blocks or rocks and discuss why this was not a good way to pray. Now every family member can take a rock or block and decore/color/paint it to place on/under their pillow every day so they remember to say their prayers.

# Plant the Word In Your Heart

## July 22-28

- Song Conductor _____
- Scripture Readers _____
- Opening Prayer _____
- Lesson _____
- Treat _____
- Closing Prayer _____

## Scriptures
Alma 32-35
Kids: Alma 32:27

## Songs
"Sweet Hour of Prayer" (Hymns, no. 142).
A Child's Prayer" (Children's Songbook, 12–13).

## Discussion
Last week we learned how 'not' to pray. See Alma 31:13-25. But this week we will discuss the different times we should pray and how we 'should' pray. Read Alma 34:17-29 and discuss the different kinds of prayer we should be giving - when, where, how, etc.

## Treat Idea
Make some dirt pudding (chocolate pudding with crushed Oreos on top) and plant seeds in your dessert (little candy rolos.)

## Discussion
Read Alma 32:28 together and discuss how it must feel for those who are struggling in the church and or struggling to believe in God. If this includes you, Try the experiment and exercise a particle of faith the way Jospeph Smith did as a young boy. Pray to know what is right and do the things God commands and keep your heart open - even if it is just a small portion of your heart and all you have is the desire to believe. An experiment needs desire, curiosity, action and a little faith.

## Activity
Read Alma 32:28-43 and discuss what it means that the Word of God is like a seed. How can we plant and nourish that seed in ourselves?
Sing together 'Faith is Like a Little Seed' and hang up the printable on the next page to remind everyone that faith starts with a tiny seed - that's all you need. Try planting your own seeds.

## Videos

Reclaimed

# Faith
## is like a little
# Seed

# Look to God and Live
## July 29-August 4

- Song Conductor_____
- Scripture Readers_____
- Opening Prayer_____
- Lesson_____
- Treat_____
- Closing Prayer_____

## Scriptures
Alma 36-38
Kids Alma 35:15

## Songs
'Give,' Said the Little Stream" (Children's Songbook, 236)

## Activities
- Read Alma 37:38-47 and discuss how the 'Word of Christ' is like the Liahona.
- Hold a treasure hunt! First, read Alma 37:6-7, then look around your house for things that are small - but make big things happen. Yeast, flour, battery, seeds, car keys, special toys, etc. You can also cut the images on the next two pages and tape them around the house for your kids to find then discuss afterward.

## Discussion Q's
- What does it mean to be 'born of God'?
- What blessings do we have because of the scriptures?
- what are some small and simple things that bring you closer to Christ?

## Treat Suggestions
Make a treat that starts with small things like flour, yeast, eggs, and make something bigger and delicious.

## Quote for the Week
"Every effort to change we make—no matter how tiny it seems to us—just might make the biggest difference in our lives."
Michael A. Dunn, *Liahona*, Nov. 2021, 106–8;

## Videos

Alma Testifies to His Son

Alma the Younger Converted

# The Great Plan of Happiness
## August 5-11

- Song Conductor_____
- Scripture Readers_____
- Opening Prayer_____
- Lesson_____
- Treat_____
- Closing Prayer_____

## Scriptures
Alma 39-42
Kids: Alma 39:15

## Songs
How Great the Wisdom and the Love," Hymns, 195.
I Am like a Star" (Children's Songbook, 163),

## Q's Discussions
- Corianton - Alma's son sinned and had to repent. How do we repent? Why do we repent?
- Read pages 19–20 of For the Strength of Youth: A Guide for Making Choices. And discuss the importance of staying away from Pornography - discuss what it is, how to recognize it and what to do when you see it. (Studies show it is only a matter of 'when,' not 'if' your children will see pornography so prepare them now.)
- Watch the video 'To Look Upon' to the right and discuss how David should have reacted and what he should have done.
- Sing 'I am Like a Star' and discuss ways you can be a good example to others.
- Do your children know someone who has died? Talk about them and how they will be resurrected one day and you will get to see them again.

## Discussion Q's
- How does Christ give us hope for redemption and forgiveness for our sins?

## Treat Suggestions
Christ is like a light/example to us, and we can follow His example. Make a dessert sun/light by making banana pudding and placing it in a pie dish. Make sun rays using graham cracker rectangles.

## Videos

Alma Counsels

To Look Upon

# Stand Fast in the Faith
## August 12-18

- Song Conductor _____
- Scripture Readers _____
- Opening Prayer _____
- Lesson _____
- Treat _____
- Closing Prayer _____

## Scriptures
Alma 43-52
Kids: Alma 46:11-20

## Songs
"We are all enlisted" (Hymns, no. 250
A Mighty Fortress Is Our God," Hymns, no. 68.

## Activities
- Read Alma 46:11-20 Mormon is discussing the wars between the Nephites and Lamanites and what Moroni did. Be like Moroni (read Alma 48:17) and your own flag/Title of Liberty using paper, fabric, markers, paint, etc. Include the causes, things that are important to you. the things you will stand for.
- Watch the video 'Elder Stevenson on Fortifying Families' below, and then make a fort out of blankets and pillows.

## Discussion Q's
What can we do to be firm in the faith of Christ?

## Treat Suggestions
You can use things like fruit roll ups, graham crackers, pretzel rods and frosting - let everyone in the family make their own fortresses out of food!

## Videos

**Temptation Fades as We Seek Christ**

**Elder Stevenson on Fortifying Families**

**Captain Moroni and The Title of Liberty**

# His Marvelous Power
## August 19-25

- Song Conductor_____
- Scripture Readers_____
- Opening Prayer_____
- Lesson_____
- Treat_____
- Closing Prayer_____

## Scriptures
Alma 53-63
Kids: Alma 56:46-47

## Songs
We'll Bring the World His Truth" (Children's Songbook, 172–73).

## Story/Discussion

"…Moroni, whose army was suffering because of inadequate support from the government, wrote to Pahoran "by the way of condemnation" and accused him and his fellow leaders of thoughtlessness, slothfulness, neglect, and even being traitors.

Pahoran easily might have resented Moroni and his inaccurate allegations, but he did not. He responded compassionately and described a rebellion against the government about which Moroni was not aware. And then Pahoran declared:

"Behold, I say unto you, Moroni, that I do not joy in your great afflictions, yea, it grieves my soul. …

"… In your epistle you have censured me, but it mattereth not; I am not angry, but do rejoice in the greatness of your heart." - Meek and Lowly of Heart," Ensign or Liahona, May 2018, 32).

What do you and your family gain/learn from this story? How can we practice not jumping to conclusions and getting offended?

## Discussion Q's

- Read Alma 56:46-47 and talk about what the young men of Helaman's little army must have been thinking/feeling.
- How does/do your mother/teachers teach you in the same way they taught the stripling warriors?
- How can we choose not to be angry?
- What are some examples of love/forgiveness you can think of? Share with your family.

## Videos

Drawing Upon the Power of God

Helaman and the 2,000 Warriors

# The Rock of our Redeemer
## August 26-September 1

- Song Conductor_____
- Scripture Readers_____
- Opening Prayer_____
- Lesson_____
- Treat_____
- Closing Prayer_____

## Scriptures
Helaman 1-6
Kids: Helaman 1:1, Helaman 5:12

## Songs
"I Need Thee Every Hour," Hymns, no. 98.
"The Wise Man and the Foolish Man" Children's Song Book 281

## Discussions
- Read Helaman 5:12 and talk about how the Savior is like a rock/foundation.
- Discuss the pride cycle as a family. (See graph on next page) Where do you think the world currently sits within the pride cycle? What comes next?
- What does it mean to build your foundation on the rock of the Redeemer?

## Activities
Build towers out of blocks and cotton balls - discuss why it is important to have a strong foundation as you sing 'The Wise Man and the Foolish Man" and as you try to blow down your different towers.

## Treat Suggestions
Edible Rocks
(The Savior is the rock/foundation)
Ingredients:
- 24 ounces white candy melts, white almond bark, or white chips
- 1 can (14 ounces) sweetened condensed milk
- 1 pinch of salt, optional
- ⅔ cup Oreo Cookie crumbs
- ½ teaspoon cocoa powder optional
- 1 drop red food coloring

See instructions on next page.

## Videos

A Secure Anchor

Nekphi and Lehi in Prison

# Pride Cycle

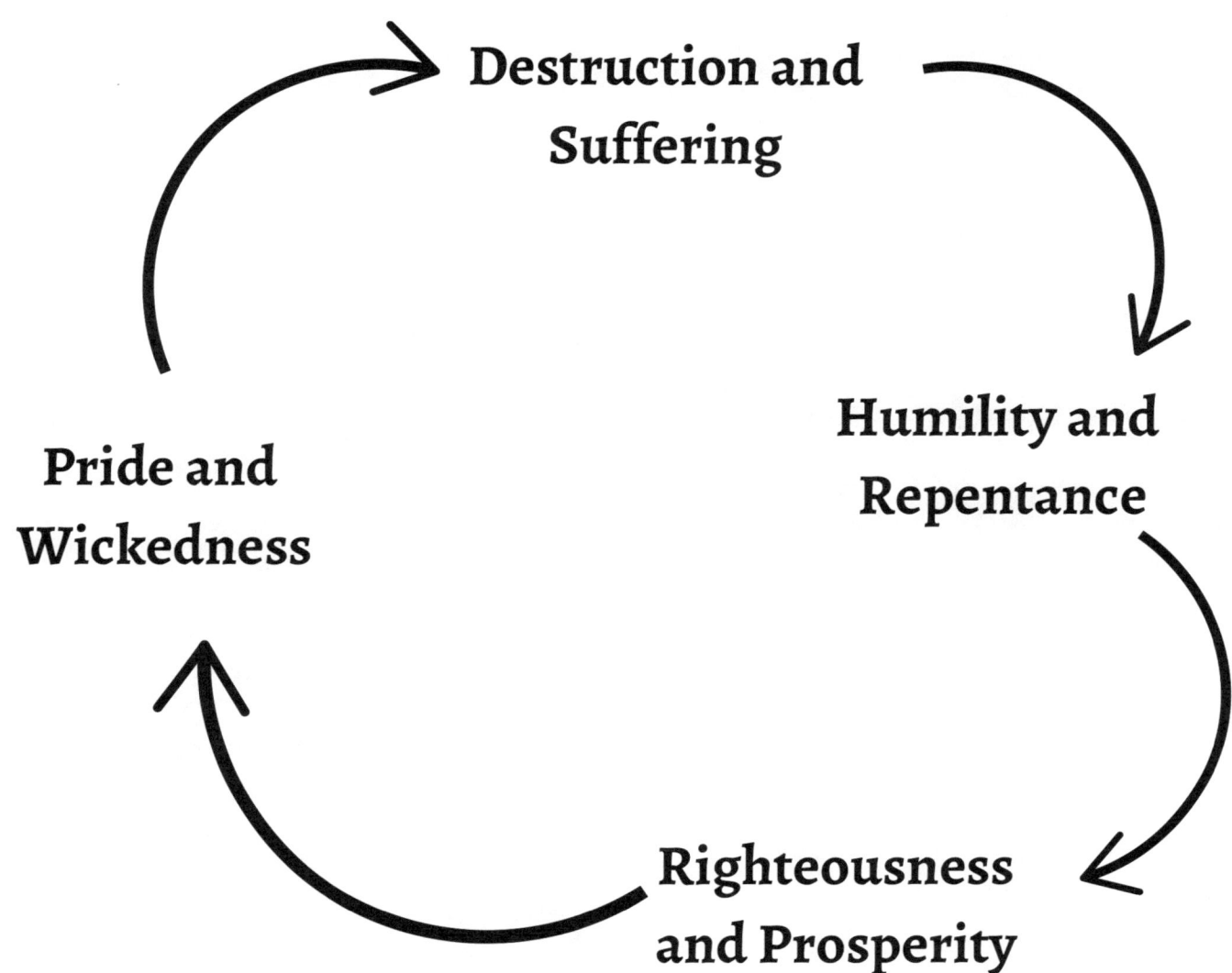

## Edible Rocks

Instructions:
1. Heat the white chocolate, sweetened condensed milk, and salt if using in a medium saucepan set over low heat stirring often until 50% melted.
2. Remove from heat and let sit for 5 minutes.
3. Add ¼ cup of the OREO cookie crumbs and stir until smooth.
4. Divide the fudge into 3 or 4 bowls and add varying amounts of the remaining cookie crumbs, cocoa powder, and red food coloring to achieve several different colors of fudge for your stones.
5. Press a piece of plastic wrap down onto the fudge in each bowl and allow it to sit at room temperature for about 30 minutes, until it is thick and no longer sticky.
6. Pinch off varying sizes of fudge, roll into odd shaped balls, and set aside to firm up.
7. Enjoy your edible rocks!

# Follow the Prophet
## September 2-8

- Song Conductor _____
- Scripture Readers _____
- Opening Prayer _____
- Lesson _____
- Treat _____
- Closing Prayer _____

## Scriptures

Helaman 7-12
Kids: Helaman 5:5-6

## Songs

"Follow the Prophet" (Children's Songbook, 110–11).

## Discussions

- Read Helaman 7:20-21 and talk about what it means to forget God.
- Sing the song recommended above then discuss our current Prophet and how he teaches/testifies of Christ.

## Treat Suggestions

Make/buy cupcakes for the footprint cupcake walk!

## Activity Idea

Cut out the footprints on the following pages and take turns writing things we can do that will help us to follow the prophet on each footprint. Place them in a circle and sing the song 'Follow the Prophet' while everyone walks around in a circle following the footprints. Play this like a cake walk - each footprint is numbered, when you stop singing draw a number from a bowl/hat and the person standing on the matching footprint gets to read it and wins a cupcake. Keep playing until everyone wins a cupcake.

## Quote for the Week

"A prophet does not stand between you and the Savior. Rather, he stands beside you and points the way to the Savior."

(Elder Neil L. Andersen *Ensign* or *Liahona*, May 2018, 26).

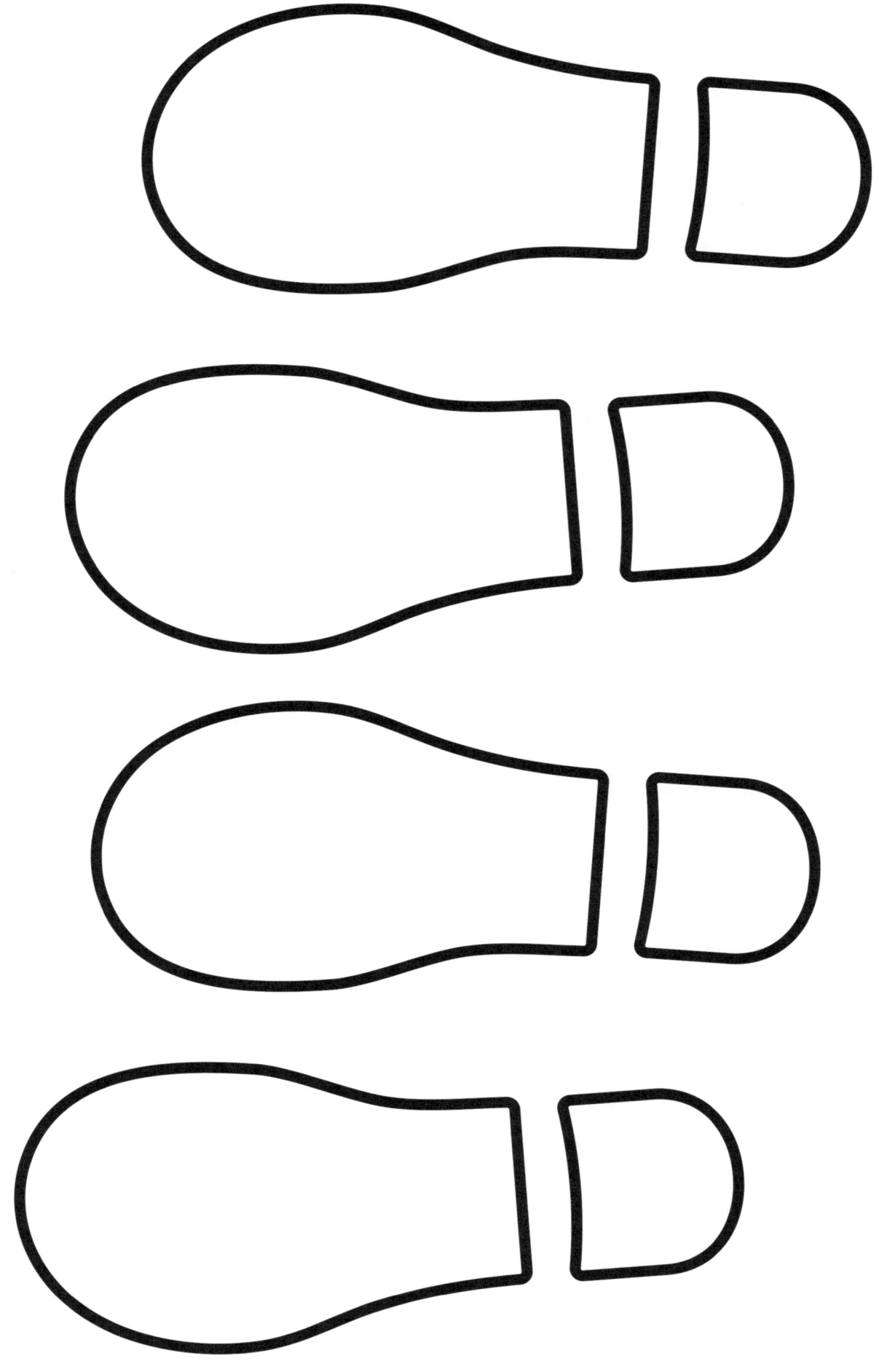

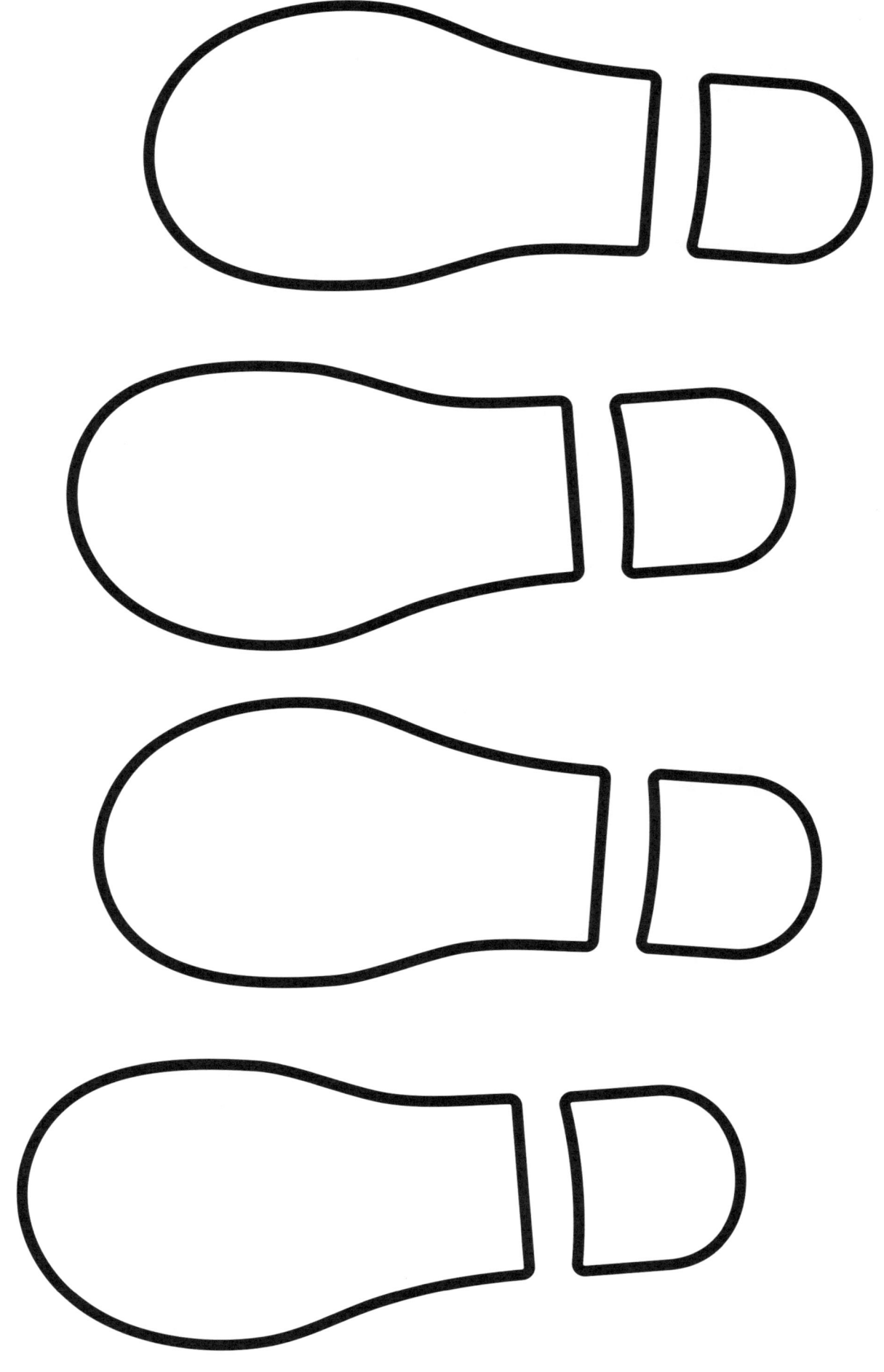

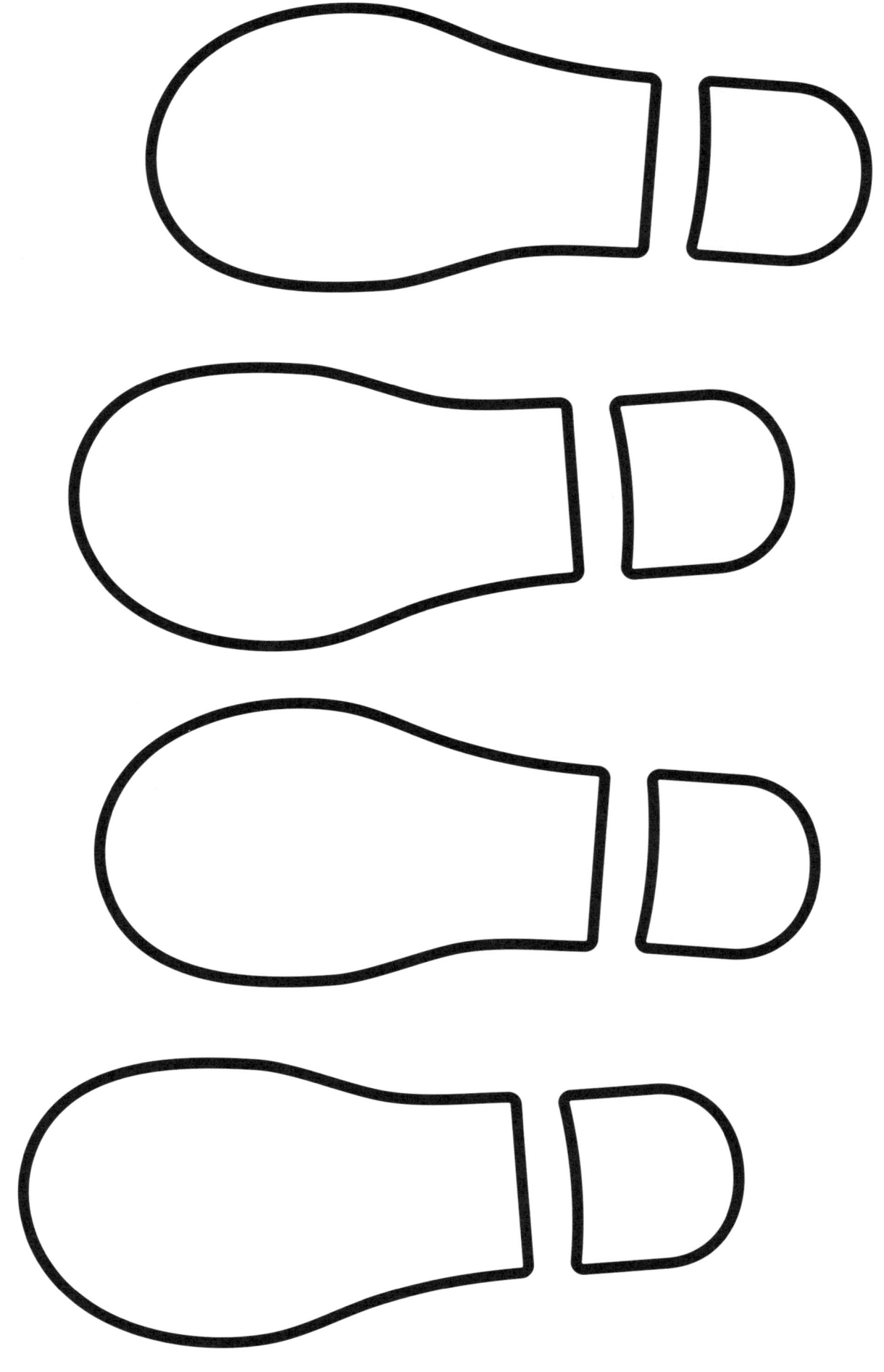

# Glad Tidings of Joy
## September 9-15

- Song Conductor_____
- Scripture Readers_____
- Opening Prayer_____
- Lesson_____
- Treat_____
- Closing Prayer_____

## Scriptures
Helaman 13-16

## Songs
"How Gentle God's Commands" (Hymns, no. 125).

## Activities
- Talk about different ways people communicate with each other - then talk about the differnet ways God communicates with us.
- How can we practicing listening to the still small voice of the spirit?

## Discussion Q's
- What is repentance?
- Why do we need to repent?
- How is repentance different from simply changing our behavior?

## Treat Suggestions
"Book of Mormon Stories," Children's Songbook 118-19

## Videos

Repentance A Joyful Choice

Principles of Peace: Repentance

Samuel the Lamanite Tells about Jesus

# Be of Good Cheer
## September 16-22

- Song Conductor_____
- Scripture Readers_____
- Opening Prayer_____
- Lesson_____
- Treat_____
- Closing Prayer_____

## Scriptures

3 Nephi 1-7
Kids: 3 Nephi 5:13

## Songs

I'm Trying to Be like Jesus," Children's Songbook, 78.

## Discussion Q's

- As a family, read through the following scriptures (Matthew 14:24–27; John 16:33; Doctrine and Covenants 61:36; 78:17–19) highlighting the places that say 'be of good cheer' Now discuss what you think that means.
- How does the Savior help us face our fears?
- What does it mean to be a disciple of Christ?
- Why is it important for us to gather together in church and as families?

## Activity

Gather a bunch of pencils or sticks. Give one to each of your your children and ask them to break them. It breaks easily because it is alone. What about when you try to break a bunch of them all together? When we stand together in unity it is harder to break the group.

## Activity

Read 3 Nephi 5:13 then trace your handprint and cut it out. Now write different ways you can be a disciple of Christ on your handprint.

## Videos

Signs of Christ's Birth

# Arise and Come Forth
## September 23-29

- Song Conductor_____
- Scripture Readers_____
- Opening Prayer_____
- Lesson_____
- Treat_____
- Closing Prayer_____

## Scriptures
3 Nephi 8-11
Kids: 3 Nephi 9:18

## Songs
"This Is My Beloved Son," Children's Songbook, 76;

## Discussion Q's
- Read 3 Nephi 9:18 and discuss what it means when Christ introduces himself as the light and the life of the world?
- How has Christ been a light in your life?
- What does it mean to give a broken heart and a contrite spirit?
- Why does Jesus want us to be baptized?

## Activity
Talk about the scriptures for the week in a darkened room and discuss what it must have been like to be in darkness for three days.

## Treat Suggestions
Get some Pirouline cookies and make them look like candles with the little flame graphics on the next page. Talk about how Jesus is the light of the world then eat the cookies.

## Quote for the Week
"That appearance and that declaration," constituted the focal point, the supreme moment, in the entire history of the Book of Mormon. It was the manifestation and the decree that had informed and inspired every Nephite prophet. … Everyone had talked of him, sung of him, dreamed of him, and prayed for his appearance—but here he actually was. The day of days! The God who turns every dark night into morning light had arrived" (Christ and the New Covenant [1997], 250–51).

## Videos

Jesus Appears Ancient Americas

# I am the Law and the Light
## September 30-October 6

- Song Conductor_____
- Scripture Readers_____
- Opening Prayer_____
- Lesson_____
- Treat_____
- Closing Prayer_____

## Scriptures
3 Nephi 12-16
Kids: 3 Nephi 15:9

## Songs
"Lord, I Would Follow Thee," Hymns, no. 220;
"I Am like a Star" (Children's Songbook, 163).

## Activities
- As a family, read 3 Nephi 12:48 as well as Jeffrey R. Holland's message "Be Ye Therefore Perfect—Eventually" (Ensign or Liahona, Nov. 2017, 40–42) Discuss what it means to be perfect - eventually.
- Read 3 Nephi 12:14–16 together and talk about how you can be an example to others. Now sing 'I am Like a Star' and have a glow in the dark hunt - buy some glow sticks and hide them around the house - turn all the lights off and hunt for the lights.

## Treat Suggestions
Read 3 Nephi 13:19-21 and discuss what it means to lay up treasures in heaven.
Have everyone in the family list outloud the treasures they would like to lay up in heaven - for each answer they get a gold chocolate coin.
Or, you can have a chocolate coin treasure hunt/scavenger hunt and when you get to the end talk about the treasures we should be focusing on during this life.

## Quote for the Week
"Brothers and sisters, every one of us aspires to a more Christlike life than we often succeed in living. If we admit that honestly and are trying to improve, we are not hypocrites; we are human. May we refuse to let our own mortal follies, and the inevitable shortcomings of even the best men and women around us, make us cynical about the truths of the gospel, the truthfulness of the Church, our hope for our future, or the possibility of godliness. If we persevere, then somewhere in eternity our refinement will be finished and complete." Elder Jeffrey R. Holland

## Videos

Jesus Teaches the Higher Law

# Behold, My Joy is Full
## October 7-13

- Song Conductor_____
- Scripture Readers_____
- Opening Prayer_____
- Lesson_____
- Treat_____
- Closing Prayer_____

## Scriptures
3 Nephi 17-19
Kids: 3 Nephi 18:24

## Songs
"As Now We Take the Sacrament," Hymns, no. 169; "A Child's Prayer" (*Children's Songbook*, 12–13),

## Activities
- Everyone in the family draw a picture of yourself with Jesus. What do imagine him doing with you? Praying with you? eating with you? teaching you?
- Read 3 Nephi 18:18-21 and sing 'A Child's Prayer' then discuss how and why we pray. What does Heavenly Father promise us about prayer?

## Discussion Q's
- How can I focus on the Savior more during the sacrament?
- Read 3 Nephi 19:9 and discuss why the gift of the Holy Ghost is so desirable.

## Quote
Our modified Sunday service is to emphasize the sacrament of the Lord's Supper as the sacred, acknowledged focal point of our weekly worship experience. - Jeffrey R. Holland

## Videos

Jesus has Compassion and Heals

Jesus Introduces Sacrament

Jesus Prays, Angels Minister to Children

# Family Trees and Tithing
## October 14-20

- **Song Conductor** _____
- **Scripture Readers** _____
- **Opening Prayer** _____
- **Lesson** _____
- **Treat** _____
- **Closing Prayer** _____

## Scriptures
3 Nephi 20-26
Kids: Mark 12:41-44

## Songs
Families Can Be Together Forever," Children's Songbook, 188.

## Activities/Discussion Q's

- Read 3 Nephi 23:1, 5 and discuss how searching is different from simply reading.

- How can we search the scriptures?

- Use pieces of pie or play money to discuss the importance of tithing and figuring out how much tithing you would have to give depending on how much your are given.

- Talk about the importance of family and family history and have your kids help you fill out the family tree on the next few pages.

## Treat Suggestions
As you work on your family trees - you can also make family tree treats!

Ingredients:
- Graham Crackers
- Frosting
- M&M's

Instructions:
Cut the graham crackers into tree-shaped triangles. Then let the kids drizzle on frosting and place an M&M for each family member you add to your family tree. Now you can eat and enjoy!

## Videos

The Refiner's Fire

Jesus Teaches - The Widows Mite

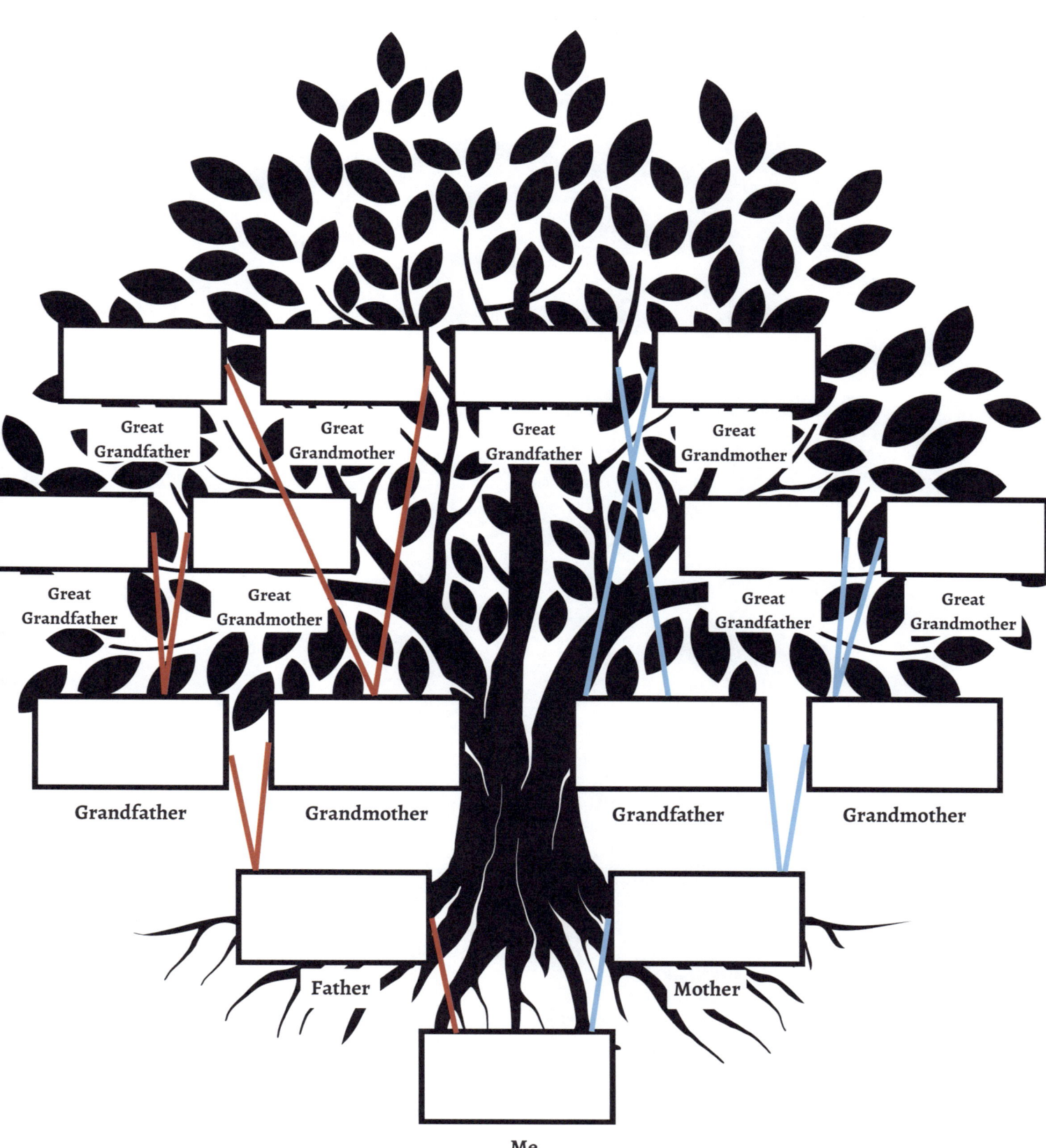

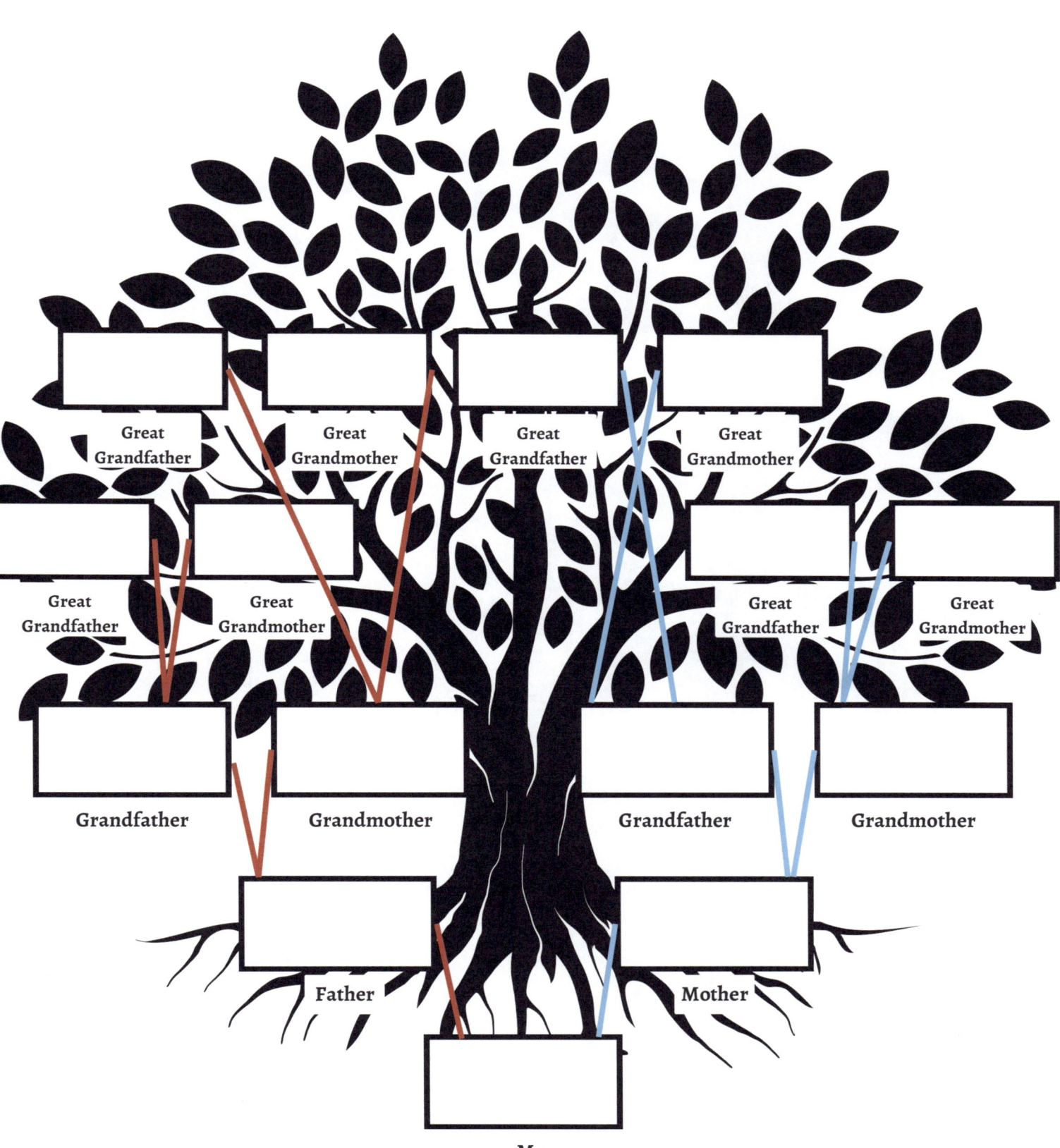

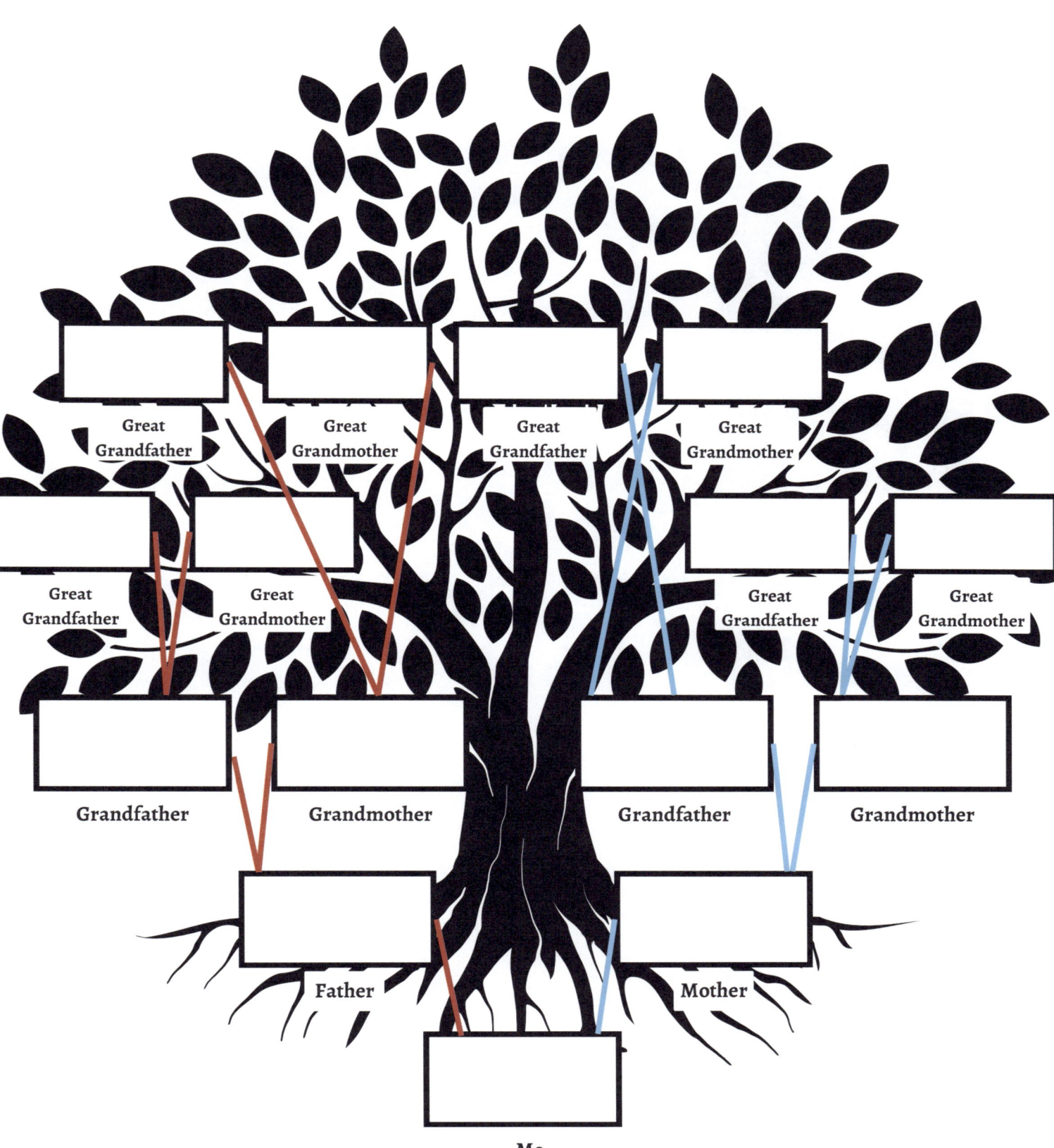

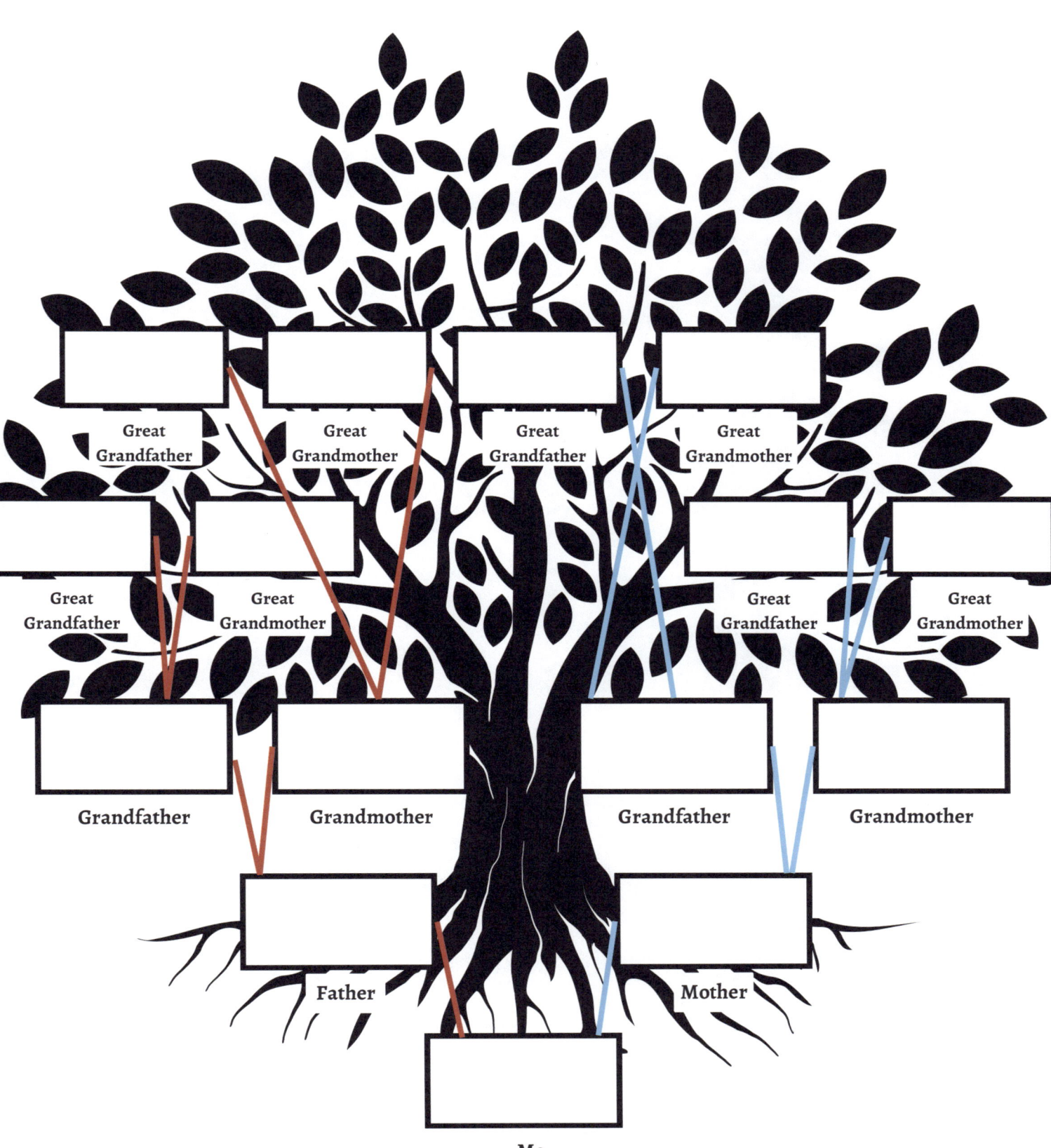

# A Happy People
## October 21-27

- Song Conductor _____
- Scripture Readers _____
- Opening Prayer _____
- Lesson _____
- Treat _____
- Closing Prayer _____

## Scriptures
3 Nephi 27 - 4 Nephi
Kids: Doctrine and Covenants 115:4

## Songs
"The Church of Jesus Christ" (Children's Songbook, 77)

## Discussion Q's
- Read 4 Nephi 1:3 and 4 Nephi 1:15-16 and talk about how all these things happened after Christ ministered to the people. What would it have been like to be some of those people?
- Read and discuss D&C 115:4. Why is it important that we use the full name of the church?
- Read 3 Nephi 27:5-8 and talk about why names are important. Why is it important that we take on ourselves the name of Christ?

## Quote for the Week
"My dear brothers and sisters, I promise you that if we will do our best to restore the correct name of the Lord's Church, He whose Church this is will pour down His power and blessings upon the heads of the Latter-day Saints, the likes of which we have never seen. We will have the knowledge and power of God to help us take the blessings of the restored gospel of Jesus Christ to every nation, kindred, tongue, and people and to prepare the world for the Second Coming of the Lord. So, what's in a name? When it comes to the name of the Lord's Church, the answer is "Everything!" Jesus Christ directed us to call the Church by His name because it is His Church, filled with His power."
-Russell M. Nelson

## Videos

The Name of the Church

Peace in America

# Repentance, Love Everyone
## October 28 - November 3

- Song Conductor_____
- Scripture Readers_____
- Opening Prayer_____
- Lesson_____
- Treat_____
- Closing Prayer_____

## Scriptures
Mormon 1-6
Kids: Mormon 3:21-22

## Songs
"Come unto Jesus," Hymns, no. 117.
"Jesus Said Love Everyone" (Children's Songbook, 61),

## Discussion Q's

- Read Mormon 3:3, 9 and discuss how you acknowledge God's influence in your life. What happens when you don't acknowledge God's influence?
- Make a list or draw pictures of the different blessings you have received from God.
- What can we do to show Heavenly Father we are grateful for our blessings?

## Activities

Read Mormon 3:12 and sing 'Jesus Said Love Everyone' and discuss what it means to love the way Jesus loves.

As a family, choose a friend or ward member you think could use some love and use the hearts on the next few pages to write nice messages and 'heart attack their house/door. You could also make some goodies as a snack for the night and to deliver with your hearts/messages.

## Videos

Mormon Preserves the Record

Something Different About Us

Mormon and His Teachings

# Faith to Move Mountains
## November 4-10

- Song Conductor_____
- Scripture Readers_____
- Opening Prayer_____
- Lesson_____
- Treat_____
- Closing Prayer_____

## Scriptures

Mormon 7-9

## Songs

"I Believe in Christ," Hymns, no. 134.
"Stand for the Right" (Children's Songbook, 159)

## Discussion Q's/Activities

- Read Mormon 7:8 and discuss. What does it mean to 'lay hold upon the gospel of Christ'?
- Talk about the different articles of faith and spend some time as a family memorizing.
- Talk about different instances where you have to choose between right and wrong - discuss the reasons this can be easy or difficult.
- Make a puzzle out of the 8'th article of faith, put it together and then have a competition to see who can memorize it first.

## Treat Suggestions

### No-Bake-Mountains

- Find/use your favorite recipe for no-bake chocolate cookies.
- Once they are finished plop spoon-fulls of the dough onto a cookie sheet as usual then shape them into tiny mountains.
- Once they are set, dust the tops with powdered sugar to look like the snow on top of a mountain.
- Use green frosting along the bottom to look like trees/grass.

## Quote for the Week

Faith in Jesus Christ is the greatest power available to us in this life. All things are possible to them that believe.
Your growing faith in Him will move mountains—not the mountains of rock that beautify the earth but the mountains of misery in your lives. Your flourishing faith will help you turn challenges into unparalleled growth and opportunity.
- Russell M. Nelson

## Videos

All May Know the Truth

# Rend the Veil of Unbelief
## November 11-17

- Song Conductor _____
- Scripture Readers _____
- Opening Prayer _____
- Lesson _____
- Treat _____
- Closing Prayer _____

## Scriptures
Ether 1-5
Kids: Ether 4:15

## Songs
"Secret Prayer," Hymns, no. 144.

## Activities

- Read Ether 4:15 and discuss what it means to 'rend the veil of unbelief' in your life.
- Read Ether 2:16-17 together while you build some of your own barges. You can use craft items from around the house like toilet paper rolls, colored paper, tape, glue, foam, pipe cleaners, popsicle sticks, clay, etc.

## Treat Suggestions
### Barges
Make little barges on the water.
Ingredients:
- Blue Jello
- Oranges
- Paper
- Toothpicks
- Clear Cups

Instructions:
- Make blue Jello and pour it into some clear cups
- While the Jello sets make tiny boats out of orange wedges
- Now make sails out of paper and toothpicks. (Cut triangles and glue the two pieces of triangle paper together onto the toothpick.

## Videos

The Jaredites Leave Babel

# Thankful, Grateful, Blessed

## November 18-24

- Song Conductor_____
- Scripture Readers_____
- Opening Prayer_____
- Lesson_____
- Treat_____
- Closing Prayer_____

## Scriptures

Ether 6-11

## Songs

"My Heavenly Father Loves Me" (Children's Songbook, 195).

## Activities

- Use the next couple pages to write down the things you are grateful/thankful for during the week.
- If your family celebrates thanksgiving you can make handprint turkeys and write something you are thankful for on each feather.

## Discussion Q's

Talk about how everyone has hard days, discuss different ways God has helped you during some hard times.

## Treat Suggestions

Friendsgiving/Service

Hold a friendsgiving with friends and family where everyone brings a dish to share, play games, and have fun!

## Quote for the Week

"God's greatest reward goes to those who serve without expectation of reward."
**Dieter F. Uchtdorf**

_____ Date_____

*Today I am Thankful for...*

_____
_____
_____
_____
_____
_____
_____
_____
_____
_____

DATE _____

*Today I am Thankful for...*

_____
_____
_____
_____
_____
_____
_____
_____
_____
_____

_____  Date_____

## Today I am Thankful for...

_____
_____
_____
_____
_____
_____
_____
_____
_____
_____

_____  Date _____

## Today I am Thankful for...

_____
_____
_____
_____
_____
_____
_____
_____
_____
_____

_____ DATE _____

## Today I am Thankful for...

_____
_____
_____
_____
_____
_____
_____
_____
_____

_____ DATE _____

## Today I am Thankful for...

_____ Date_____

## Today I am Thankful for...

_____
_____
_____
_____
_____
_____
_____
_____
_____

# Anchor of Hope
## November 25 - December 1

- **Song Conductor** _____
- **Scripture Readers** _____
- **Opening Prayer** _____
- **Lesson** _____
- **Treat** _____
- **Closing Prayer** _____

## Scriptures
Ether 12-16
Kids: Ether 12:5-6

## Songs
"The Lord Is My Light," Hymns, no. 89.

## Activities
Why do boats need anchors? What would happen to a boat that does not have an anchor? As you read Ether 12:4 together, talk about how hope helps us the way an anchor helps a boat while you color the anchors on the next few pages.

## Discussion Q's
Read Ether 12:5-6 and discuss. What is faith? How do we exercise our faith?
Read Ether 12:27 and talk about how we can come to the Savior to make our weaknesses become strong.

## Treat Suggestions
Make Rice Krispy treats and shape them to look like anchors.

## Quote for the Week
"So, when our backs are to the wall and, as the hymn says, "other helpers fail and comforts flee," among our most indispensable virtues will be this precious gift of hope linked inextricably to our faith in God and our charity to others."

*A Perfect Brightness of Hope*
**By Elder Jeffrey R. Holland**

# Going to Church
## December 2-8

- Song Conductor_____
- Scripture Readers_____
- Opening Prayer_____
- Lesson_____
- Treat_____
- Closing Prayer_____

## Scriptures
Moroni 1-6
Kids: Moroni 6:1-3

## Songs
"In Memory of the Crucified" (Hymns, no. 190).
"Reverently, Quietly," Children's Songbook, 26).

## Activities
- Read Moroni 6:4-6,9 and talk about the important things we do at church.
- Everyone in the family draw the thing you enjoy most about going to church.
- How can we 'as a family' work together to keep the sabbath day holy?

## Discussion Q's
Read Moroni 4:3 and 5:2 and work on memorizing the sacrament prayers.
Why is it important to be reverant during the sacrament?

## Treat Suggestions
Maybe as a family you could make bread to donate for the church to use as the sacrament bread.

## Strengthening New Members (Videos)

Working Together

The Importance of Friendships

The Bush Family Story

Use My Covenant Path

# May Christ Lift Thee Up
## December 9-15

- Song Conductor _____
- Scripture Readers _____
- Opening Prayer _____
- Lesson _____
- Treat _____
- Closing Prayer _____

## Scriptures

Moroni 7-9
Kids: Moroni 7:3

## Songs

"Love One Another," Hymns, no. 308;

## Discussion Q's/Activities

- Read Moroni 7:47 and talk about what it means to have 'Charity.' Have your children draw pictures of what they think it looks like when they are being charitable/loving/Christlike to others.
- What are some ways Jesus showed love to others?
- Read Moroni 7:20 and discuss what it means to lay hold upon every good thing.

## Quote for the Week

"I plead with you to control your tempers, to put a smile upon your faces, which will erase anger; speak out with words of love and peace, appreciation, and respect. If you will do this, your lives will be without regret. Your marriages and family relationships will be preserved. You will be much happier. You will do greater good. You will feel a sense of peace that will be wonderful.

May the Lord bless you and inspire you to walk without anger, without bitterness of any kind, but to reach out to others with expressions of friendship, appreciation, and love."

Slow To Anger - **Gordon B. Hinckley**

## Videos

Patterns of Light

Charity: An Example of the Believers

# Come Unto Christ
## December 16-22

- Song Conductor_____
- Scripture Readers_____
- Opening Prayer_____
- Lesson_____
- Treat_____
- Closing Prayer_____

## Scriptures

Moroni 10
Kids: Moroni 10:32

## Songs

"Let the Holy Spirit Guide," Hymns, no. 143;
"Search, Ponder, and Pray" (Children's Songbook, 109).

## Activities/Discussion Q's

- Read Moroni 10:8 and discuss the different gifts/talents the members of your family have been blessed with. Children can draw pictures of their gifts.
- Read Moroni 10:3-4 and talk to your kids about how they can ask to know if the Book of Mormon is true for themselves.
- Color and cut the heart badges on the next page.

## Activities

Write out the different gifts on slips of paper from Moroni 10:9-16. Wrap them like little gifts and have your family take turns opening and discussing each gift.

## Treat Suggestions

Make heart shaped cookies and talk about the different ways we show God that we love Him.

## Videos

Moroni Invites all to Come Unto Christ

The Promise of the Book of Mormon

## Quote for the Week

A keystone is a wedge-shaped stone at the top of an arch that locks the other stones together. To help your fame at the top. What happens if the keystone is removed? WhHow can we make the Book of Mormon the keystone of our faith in Jesus Christ?

"I love God with all my might, mind, and strength"

"I love God with all my might, mind, and strength"

"I love God with all my might, mind, and strength"

"I love God with all my might, mind, and strength"

# Christmas Time
## December 23-29

- Song Conductor_____
- Scripture Readers_____
- Opening Prayer_____
- Lesson_____
- Treat_____
- Closing Prayer_____

## Songs

"Stars Were Gleaming" (Children's Songbook, 37)
"Picture a Christmas" (Children's Songbook, 50)
"Away in a Manger," Hymns, no. 206.
"He Sent His Son" (Children's Songbook, 34–35)

## Discussion/Activities

- Have your children make a book of drawings depicting the birth of Jesus Christ. You can use the print out on the next page to read the christmas story together while they draw.
- Discuss your favorite Book of Mormon story that you studied in the last year.

## Activities

Use the Christmas activity pages following this page.

## Treat Suggestions

Make Christmas cookies, gingerbread houses, or other festive treats.

## Videos

The Christ Child

He is the Gift

Give as Jesus Gave

Light the World with Service

# THE Nativity

1. And it came to pass in those days, that there went out a decree from Cæsar Augustus, that all the world should be taxed.

2. (And this taxing was first made when Cyrenius was governor of Syria.)

3. And all went to be taxed, every one into his own city.

4. And Joseph also went up from Galilee, out of the city of Nazareth, into Judæa, unto the city of David, which is called Bethlehem; (because he was of the house and lineage of David:)

5. To be taxed with Mary his espoused wife, being great with child.

6. And so it was, that, while they were there, the days were accomplished that she should be delivered.

7. And she brought forth her firstborn son, and wrapped him in swaddling clothes, and laid him in a manger; because there was no room for them in the inn.

8. And there were in the same country shepherds abiding in the field, keeping watch over their flock by night.

9. And, lo, the angel of the Lord came upon them, and the glory of the Lord shone round about them: and they were sore afraid.

10. And the angel said unto them, Fear not: for, behold, I bring you good tidings of great joy, which shall be to all people.

11. For unto you is born this day in the city of David a Saviour, which is Christ the Lord.

12. And this shall be a sign unto you; Ye shall find the babe wrapped in swaddling clothes, lying in a manger.

13. And suddenly there was with the angel a multitude of the heavenly host praising God, and saying,

14. Glory to God in the highest, and on earth peace, good will toward men.

15. And it came to pass, as the angels were gone away from them into heaven, the shepherds said one to another, Let us now go even unto Bethlehem, and see this thing which is come to pass, which the Lord hath made known unto us.

16. And they came with haste, and found Mary, and Joseph, and the babe lying in a manger.

LUKE 2

# Count Our Blessings Tree

1. **Print the 'Blessings Tree' and 'Blessings Ornaments' found on the following few pages.**
2. **Cut the ornaments out, and hang your tree somewhere; the whole family will see it daily. (Or print one journal for each family member, so everyone has their own tree and journal pages.)**
3. **Each day during the month (or 12 days, or week) before Christmas, every family member can choose an ornament that lists a blessing he or she is grateful for and add it to the tree.**

# Blessings Ornaments

| | | | | |
|---|---|---|---|---|
| Family | Home | Love | Faith | Books |
| Food | Toys | Warmth | Pizza | Ice Cream |
| God | Jesus | My Body | Trees | School |
| Earth | Father | Sister | Brother | Mother |

# Blessings Ornaments

- WORDS
- FRIENDS
- LOVE
- VILLAGE
- SPORTS
- CANDY
- LIFE
- OUTSIDE
- SPORTS
- GRASS
- COMMUNITY
- THE SUN
- FLOWERS
- TREES
- THE MOON
- PAPER
- SUGAR
- HEALTH
- SPICE
- STARS

# Blessings Ornaments

- GAMES
- STORIES
- LOVE
- HOME
- ROOF
- CAR
- COUSINS
- GRANDMA
- OUTSIDE
- FIRE
- MOBILITY
- HOPE
- ANIMALS
- WATER
- SUGAR
- PETS
- A ROOM
- A BED
- PARENTS
- CHURCH

# Make Your Own Blessings Ornaments

# Christmas Service

Help make baby Jesus's bed soft and cozy by adding a bundle of straw to the manger every time you perform an act of service.

1. **Print the 'Manger Made of Service' on the next page and the 'Acts of Service' Straw bundles on the following few pages.**
2. **Every time someone in the family performs an act of service, cut out that bundle of straw and add it to the manger (using glue or tape.)**
3. **Once the manger is full of straw, put the baby Jesus in His bed on Christmas morning.**

# A Manger Made of Love and Service

# Baby Jesus

# Acts of Service Straw

- Made My Bed
- Clean My Room
- Put Away Clothes
- Share
- Give A Back Rub
- Give A Compliment
- Wash Dishes
- Help Shovel Snow
- Donate
- Share Toys
- Help A Friend
- Babysit

# Acts of Service Straw

- Give a Gift
- Make a Gift
- Make & Share a Treat
- Plant Flowers
- Sing Carols
- Donate to Local Food Bank
- Clean a Local Park
- Pick Up Litter
- Volunteer
- Host a Dog Wash
- Host a Carwash for Charity
- Bake Sale for Charity

# Acts of Service Straw

- Visit elderly home
- Go caroling
- Make & share a treat
- Make fleece blankets to donate
- Teach someone something
- Organize a food drive
- Clean a local park
- Pick up litter
- Donate books
- Write thank you notes
- Smile at someone
- Give a hug

# Acts of Service Straw (Make Your Own)

**Christmas Handouts**

**Christmas Handouts**

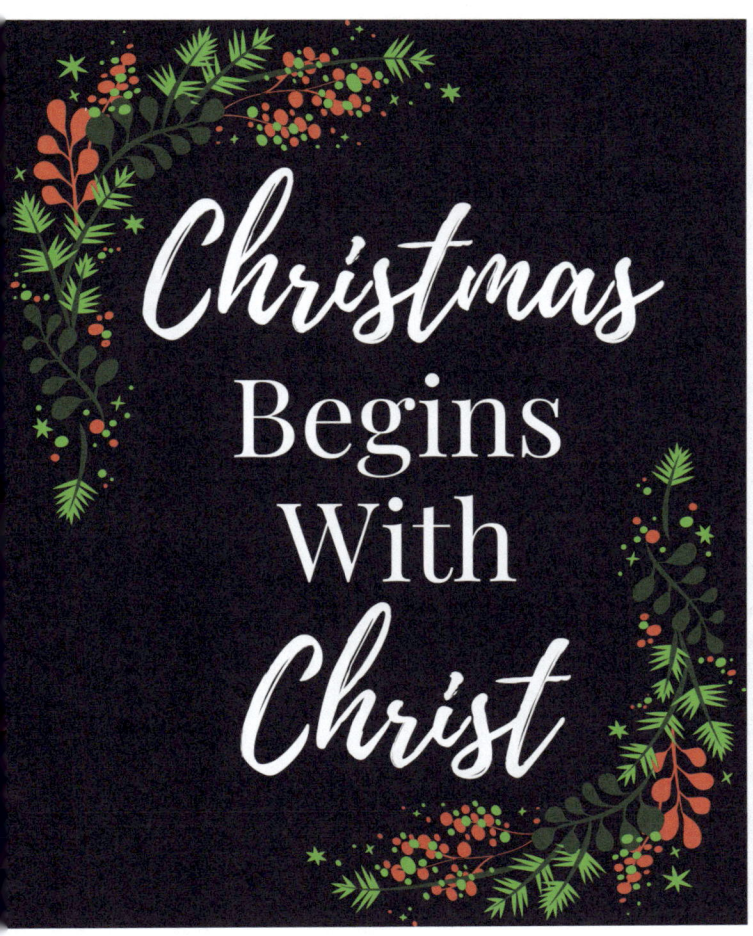

Made in United States
Troutdale, OR
01/02/2024

16617771R00100